Habitat Hoodrat: Ho-Nation

Harm City U.S.A: Winter 2015-16

**Welcome to Baltimore,
Known to the Victims of Your Privilege Who Live
Here as "Harm City"**

Harm City is the beating moral heart of the
Maryland Income Redistribution Region.

Are you weary of taking, and taking?

Are you of a mind to give back to those who have
suffered so that you might thrive?

Then enter this node of Habitat Hoodrat...

Privileged Zone (Blue)

If you would like to shoulder your social
responsibility and at the same time serve as an
example to the less fortunate, feel free to buy,
rent or tour in a Privilege Zone, confident that the
most progressive tax code in the United States
will absolve you of that nagging intergenerational
guilt.

Opportunity Zone (Yellow)

If you would prefer to experience direct giving,
access an Opportunity Zone, and enjoy giving to
our Regan Era Homeless Re-enactors, conveniently

posted on street corners and freeway access ramps.

Entitlement Zone (Red)

If you would prefer the thrill of a suspenseful and guilt-abolishing wealth transfer, visit an Entitlement Zone, wherein you might be relieved of your burden by hard working facilitators and possibly have your heroic giving experience immortalized as a Hip Hop video upload.

Welcome to Harm City, Maryland

About the Cover

Ho-Nation by Black Jamaican Nazi, Oliver
Wendell Hayes

Hey James,

"I couldn't do as elaborate a photoshop as I wanted to
because apparently there is a shortage of high
quality/resolution face forward pictures of hood rats on the
we (apparently they don't like being photographed, which
is what I'd need to render a good animal transformation in
ps. Hopefully this will do, If not please don't hesitate to say
as I'm already working on a couple alternatives. The
background in this picture is local, @ North Ave. & Belair
Road. It is also already at 350 dpi."

Books by James LaFond

Nonfiction
The Fighting Edge, 2000
The Logic of Steel, 2001
The First Boxers, 2011
The Gods of Boxing, 2011
All Power Fighting, 2011
When You're Food, 2011
The Lesser Angles of Our
Nature, 2012
The Logic of Force, 2012
The Greatest Boxer, 2012
Take Me to Your Breeder, 2014
The Streets Have Eyes, 2014
Panhandler Nation, 2014
The Ghetto Grocer, 2014
American Fist, 2014
Don't Get Boned, 2014
Alienation Nation, 2014
In The Chinks of The Machine,
2014
How the Ghetto Got My Soul,
2014
Saving the World Sucks, 2014
Taboo You, 2014
The Fighting Life, 2014
Narco Night Train, 2014
Into the Mountains of Madness:
in [3 volumes], 2014
Incubus of Your Sacred
Emasculation, 2014
Breeder's Digest, 2014
The Third Eye, 2015
Modern Agonistics, 2015
By the Wine Dark Sea, 2015
The Pale Usher, 2016
The End of Masculine Time,
2015
War Drums, 2015
A Thousand Years in His Soul:
The Poets, 2015
A Thousand Years in His Soul:
The Seers, 2015
Of Lions and Men, 2015
Your Trojan Whorse, 2016
On Bitches, 2016

Equidistant Drowning Babies,
2015
The Boned Zone, 2015
A Sickness of the Heart: Part
One, 2015
Let the Weak Fall, 2015
If I Were King, 2015
Dark Art of an Aryan Mystic,
2015
Welcome to Harm City: White
Boy, 2015
When You're Food: Raw, 2016
No B.S. Boxing, 2016
Stick Fighting Fundamentals,
2016
Our Captain, 2016
Stillbirth of A Nation, 2016
America in Chains, 2106
40,000 Years from Home, 2016
The Sardonyx Stone, 2016
Neanderthal Resistance, 2016
A Dread Grace, 2016
Habitat Hoodrat, 2016
The Poor Tour/Ghetto Gourmet,
2016
40,000 Years from Home, 2016
A Once Great Medieval City,
2016
A Thousand Years in His Soul,
2016
The Liver-Eater Reader, 2016
Why Grownups Suck, 2016

Fiction
Astride the Chariot of Night,
2014
Sacrifix, 2014
Rise, 2014
Motherworld, 2014
Planet Buzzkill, 2014
Fruit of The Deceiver, 2014
Forty Hands of Night, 2014
Black and Pale, 2014
Daughters of Moros, 2014
Darkly, 2014

Habitat Hoodrat: Ho-Nation

This Design is Called Paisley, 2015
Hurt Stoker, 2015
Poet, 2016
Triumph, 2015
Winter, 2015
The Spiral Case, 2015
Hemavore, with Dominick Mattero, 2016
Yusuf of the Dusk, 2016
Beyond the Pale, 2016
RetroGenesis: Day 1, with Erique Watson, 2015
Easy Chair, 2015
Happily Ever Under, 2015
Road Killing, 2015
Fat Girl Dancing, 2015
Buzz Bunny, 2015
T. Spoone Slickens, Inquire, 2015
Dream Flower, 2015
The Song of Jeannot, 2015
Organa, 2015
A Hoodrat Halloween, 2015
Buzz Bunny, 2015
The Consultant, 2015
Reverent Chandler, 2015

He, 2016
Little Feet Going Nowhere, 2016
DoomFawn, 2016
The Jericho Bone, 2016
Ire and Ice, 2016
Under the Crescent, 2016

Sunset Saga Novels
Big Water Blood Song, 2011
Ghosts of the Sunset World, 2011
Beyond the Ember Star, 2012
Comes the Six Winter Night, 2012
Thunder-Boy, 2012
The World is Our Widow, 2013
Behind the Sunset Veil, 2013
Den of The Ender, 2013
God's Picture Maker, 2014
Out of Time, 2015
Seven Moons Deep, 2016

For "Unka" Bernie Hackett, a man cynically
beyond the reach of political correctness

Contents

'Lady Footlocker'
Inspector Ratchet Lights the Warning Torch: Mongrel Hoodrats Have Breached Yo Adrian's Wall With Combat Incubators!

"So I saw this in Baltimore......oh wait it's my local mall. Fun times ahead."

-Inspector Ratchet

Dude, my position was overrun 20 years ago! It's about time their lead elements got to you rear echelon guys!

It sounds like you have breeder active in your sector, Inspector....

Seriously, with the names and appearances of the few stories from Lancaster and environs sent by you and Nero the Pict, it seems like you have a seriously inbred Latino-African-Norway hoodrat subspecies—perhaps the one that may metastasize globally. If you could ship me a live specimen via media mail—it's cheaper—I would appreciate it, as I am soon to be beginning the Hoodrat Habitat Guide. Please, remember to poke holes in the box before you ship it out—and they eat Pop Tarts, with or without frosting. My landlord gets pissed over DOA parcels and I don't need it famished when it hops out of the box in my laboratory...

http://lancasteronline.com/news/local/girl-charged-with-assault-in-slashing-of-at-park-city/article_868529f2-a8e3-11e5-92f2-83bfec6e935b.html

Cops Can No Longer Punch in Baltimore County

Police Investigating After Video Shows Officers Punching Man Outside Towson Bar

© 2015 James LaFond

Baltimore is like a pork roast!

Can you believe those seven pitty-pat arm punches on the head are considered excessive force?

A shin kick or choke would have been more effective, but they are not allowed.

The pig should have just done a face press with both hands, grinding the guy's face into the pavement from a pushup position—oh, but that would have been too violent!

Now, I hate cops. But, if some drunken knucklehead is so out of control that he is going to pick a fight with three cops, what are you supposed to do? Short of high level grappling, there is nothing that liberals are going to allow cops to do. And since cops will never be high level grapplers, and they can no longer use weapons even in their own defense, and are barred nationally from using neck holds or chokes, than, without the latitude to strike with empty hands they will be helpless, except as a Romper Room mugging team.

By the way, the ranking police officer I am currently training is learning the palm jab and palm cross, because I don't want him breaking his trigger finger on some empty chunk of Baltimore ebony.

This is hilarious, particularly the faggot white politician. I hope that dude gets gang raped by a bunch of homeboys in the Towson Town Center parking garage.

Now, after watching the police department and the media and politicians throw this cop under the bus, do you knuckleheads who come here for training advice, think you are going to be able to get away with shooting, knifing, kicking or even punching, some similar endangered species of criminal?

Not only do we live in the insane world where the man who disbanded the KKK somehow founded the KKK in his own absence, but we also live in the kinetic fantasy realm where ineffective punches are now excessive force?

That pig could hit me on top of my head for as long as he wanted and it would have no effect on my aged braincase, let alone the mahogany dome of this dumbass.

Thanks, Tanya, for the news clip.

http://baltimore.cbslocal.com/2015/12/20/
police-investigating-after-video-shows-
officers-punching-man-outside-towson-bar/

'Safety Knowledge'
'Flushing Neighborhood Watch Team' [With Correction]

© 2015 James LaFond

In the article below I mentioned that the attacker of Yaoyu was black. Brooklyn Shane called to correct me.

"The dude that killed and raped Yaoyu was not black but of another innocent group—an illegal Mexican immigrant who had already been convicted of a crime and deported before and came back. Of course, yours was a reasonable assumption, since almost all of the multitude of violent crimes committed against Chinese in Flushing are committed by blacks from a nearby housing project. They are pretty much getting slaughtered, just no-holds barred attack after attack, almost all black on yellow. I tell my one Chinese friend that he is my replacement. That him and his people are good earners and aren't violent, so are going to be the preferred prey species in the New America."

This brochure is as black on white as a postmodern crime, with an image of a shirtless young man being KO'd by a Chinese person in traditional garb.

"Suffering Violence again and again, Keeping silence is no longer an option!"

"Maintaining security and order is everybody's duty."

"Team spirit and purpose."

According to Brooklyn Shane, who sent me this ad, this is in response to the largely Chinese community of Flushing, New York being preyed upon remorselessly by black men and youth, with a Chinese woman recently attacked by a black [correction, Mexican] man who bashed her brains out against a pipe and raped her as she died. According to Shane, this process in New York, of blacks hunting and preying upon Chinese, is decades old and intensely violent and one-sided, with large black youths ganging up on smaller, less numerous, unarmed, and often younger and female victims.

It is interesting to see such a traditional outcry against the Liberal American Paradise of Urban America. On the interior of the brochure are translated invitations to free "Kong Fu" lessons, directions to patrol in groups of five with whistles and cell phones, with additional whistles to pass out to concerned bystanders who will be directed to keep within sight of criminals and continue blowing whistles, acting as spotter hounds for the police.

Unfortunately, in Liberal Urban America, the police are being told to stand down and not arrest. A full bore propaganda campaign has been launched by The Baltimore Sun for an entire week, focusing on nothing but the helplessness of black men before drug addiction and drug trafficking, the call to house more ghetto children in affluent white suburbia, and the need to use less police action against black criminals.

New York, LA, Chicago, are not the liberal pilot plans for the war on law abiding citizens by the proxy black mob of the Left. Places like Baltimore are the test ground. I am sorry to inform these law abiding Chinese that the law is being sculpted in such a way as to completely abandon them to their fate.

The law officer of the future is nothing but an agent of citizen disarmament, which will be directed to avoid contact with unarmed violent mobs of young, unarmed, large, black criminals and persecute the small, lone, armed defender, assuring a predatory matrix that will keep the balance of the population in line.

However, I like the spirit of this Safety Knowledge brochure and would like to continue on a positive note, in their words [which is followed by a ten-step Code of Conduct]:

Line 1: "Let us draw a lesson from the bitter experience, mend the fold after the sheep is lost, [Who would not want people who see themselves as sheep as citizens?] and prevent any recurrence of the tragedy of "Yaoyu"!

Line 3; "If everyone of us is worldly-wise and plays safe, all of us will eventually suffer disaster."

Line 7: "Let us unite and get organized and show the strength of the ethnic Chinese!"

Line 11: "Let us unite and get organized, and cultivate a spirit of mutual loving care, and act bravely for a just cause."

Just in case any of you white people currently suffering the indignity of being robbed, raped, beaten and murdered by gangs of blacks, are considering banding together like the "ethnic Chinese" of Flushing, New York, keep in mind that the police will be sent against you, and if they cannot handle you, you will be doing your Kent State student protestor imitation in front of a fire team of National Guardsmen, commanded—as is the Maryland National Guard Riot Task Force—by a black female officer.

Ajay Moved Out Just In Time
Loch Hill and Hillendale Residents Under Hoodrat Assault

© 2015 James LaFond

I was missing my best friend recently, at Christmas time, when I sat down to talk with my cousin, who lives less than a mile from Ajay's recently abandoned home, who, having enough of police helicopters chasing hoodrats through her yard, recently evacuated Harm City along with a number of other friends and relatives of mine. Patty is stuck in a house that lost value in the housing crash.

Patty lives in a very nice single family home in a small all-white Baltimore County community less than a quarter mile from the city line. Until the recent riot and purge back in April, her area—not being next to subsidized housing or on a walk-through grid, but situated on a wooded hilltop with no secondary street access—had been crime free. Apparently emboldened by political-minded police showing a notable reluctance to arrest black youth, groups of teenage blacks from the York Road and McClean Boulevard crime highways [primary streets along which subsidized housing is served by bus routes, fried lake trout and fried chicken joints, hair and nail salons and liquor stores] have been prowling through the neighborhood by day and kicking in basement doors and back doors, looting in broad daylight with no apparent fear of police or reprisals.

I informed Patty that things would be getting no better, as the Baltimore County Police of the Towson Precinct have already given up that forward line of defense, and are operating primarily at the final redoubt before the I-695 loop and Loch Raven Reservoir and Gun Powder State Park, which pretty much marks the final line of resistance for white flight candidates, before they bail from the area just east of the Towson Seat of Baltimore County and flee to Harford County [which has just defeated a Wal-Mart initiative to bring up thousands of Baltimore City hoodrats] or remove themselves to the north of Yo Adrian's Wall into South-Central Pennsylvania.

Habitat Hoodrat: Ho-Nation

The hoodrat hordes are coming, with support from the Baltimore City Housing Authority, which is buying single family homes and row homes in Baltimore and Harford County, and moving single-mother welfare families from the Baltimore ghettos out to form forward logistical hubs for the intensifying war on Working America. The Baltimore County Police Force are also conspiring to keep the invasion a secret by "softening" and falsifying reports, and by neglecting to report on the rapidly expanding black-on-white crime wave in Central Maryland.

Patty told me that, due to this development, she will be voting for Trump or, if Trump bails out of the election, Cruz.

My prediction is, that if a democrat gets into the Oval Office for a third term in a row, areas like Central Maryland will erupt into a continual low-intensity Urban-on-suburban, black-on-white war, aided and abetted by police departments beholding to local media-owned politicians. The leftist media already has its propaganda machine in place, cranking out the necessary lies as I write.

In Sissy America, I think it will sell, with historians of the future having no more of a clue that the Working White People of Central Maryland lived under a silent reign of terror any more than the historians of today know that the Maryland Gazette once published weekly notices of runaway white slaves with more regularity than current ad subscribers buy space in the remaining area newspapers to advertise jobs.

'Drop-Kicking Toddlers'
Vintage Tommy Sotomayor: Mescaline Franklin's Sunday Morning Video Pick

Holy shit, A Tommy video from 2012!

This kid is Satan...drop-kicking toddlers and shit.

You know, we differ on the question of race and behavior. Even so, I give every individual an opportunity to prove to me that they deserve respect. I don't think people realize that the reason why you don't get mad or upset at most people is that you do not recognize them as human and therefore assign no agency to their actions. You see most people as domestic animals with no free will. I think Evola is the only author to the right of you. I mean, you think White Nationalists are liberals! I don't think most people realize that you're essentially a hold-over of some ancient age.

Merry Christmas!

https://www.youtube.com/watch?v=VdaKDbSpPSA

Naked in New York?
Manny's Mobile Clothing for all Occassions has you covered

Along with news of the Flushing, New York Neighborhood watch team, Brooklyn Shane mailed me an impressive coated color business card from a street clothier operating out of a van who represents name brand apparel manufacturers and sells this stuff far cheaper than traditional outlets, who apparently lack the benefit of Manny's sophisticated procurement methods.

I realize that I am guilty as coming off as anti-American and anti-materialistic. So, please, by all means embrace the Almighty God of Things and call 646-322-1657 so that Manny may roll his slice of Americana up to your residence or place of business and turn the sidewalk into a postmodern bazaar of the bizarre.

"Got yo Nikes, yo Timberlands en yo Jordans—bes prices in town—come on aroun!"

Ten Percent

The Hoodrat Assault on Melody's Neighborhood

© 2015 James LaFond

James, please do not divulge my location. I want you to know what area I live in in case it helps you with your work. Suffice it to say that I live in a Baltimore County residential community with 10% black residence. It is strange that houses that go on the market are sometimes quickly sold when others languish for years, end then a black welfare family that could never afford such a home is soon in residence. Enough of these families have materialized in the neighborhood that we have small gangs of black boys vandalizing cars, lazing along in the middle of the street on their bikes and scowling at white motorists, daring us to affirm our right of way.

My car was stoned by a group of them and my son in law got in his car and stalked them around the neighborhood. They knew what he was up to and gradually removed themselves by street and alley, until they attacked another white man's vehicle. This man was so upset by this he took one of them off of his bike and then ran over the bike with his truck. In response two white women called the police on this man and he was in deep trouble for opposing this pint-sized reign of terror.

We now have unknown—and sometimes hooded and masked—black men walking the streets menacingly.

There is a nice black woman who lives across the street, a foster mother with a retarded teenage girl—a younger teenager—who goes from yard to yard and peers within, taking inventory on a note pad! I told a woman who is in a leadership position in the neighborhood association about this and she blew it off as child's play, thinking that I was overreacting.

There is one man flying the American and Confederate flag from a pole in his yard who seems determined to resist. Thank God for him.

'The Golden Child'

Chasing A Killer by Justin Fenton in The Baltimore Sun, 12/27/15

© 2015 James LaFond

The lying, nihilistic, leftist rag that tragically passes as the journal of record in Harm City does have one real reporter on its staff. His name is Justin Fenton and he is following two black homicide detectives as they investigate the murder of a black man by two black men which was caught on film and witnessed by a dozen black people in broad daylight, just minutes after one of these detectives pulled away from that very liquor store in Northwest Baltimore during his investigation of a previous shooting.

In our sick world only the shooter is sought for this killing, with the man who set up the victim and diverted his attention as his partner pressed a pistol to the back of his head and blew his brains out perhaps sought as a witness.

The witnesses saw nothing, indeed, did not even scatter or look away as the body was dropped. As the police investigated, the locals displayed irritation with their presence and were displeased with crime scene tape blocking their access to the liquor store.

Even though the victim's older brother was once duct taped in a basement and blown apart with a shotgun by a known and un-convicted shooter, the grieving mother and family will not cooperate with the investigation.

The mother did receive 100K from The City for the death of her middle son, who attempted to run over a white police officer, who then shoot and killed him.

That is all the family cares about, that white cop.

There is one decent figure in the family, an uncle who has worked his entire life and speaks against drug dealing.

The one police detective knew the oldest brother, and both detectives knew both killers on sight, naming the shooter "The Golden Child" for he is known to have killed four people and has not suffered incarceration or conviction for these killings.

Justin Fenton's transparent writing style avoids liberal or conservative moralization and permits the reader to search the dark shadows of the sick society that is Black Baltimore on its own terms, even as other Sun staff writers launch a full-on propaganda campaign declaring the helplessness and lack of agency of black youth and men, victimized by drugs, law enforcement, the corrections system, the school system and the racism of whites.

In one of the rare solid news stories out of Baltimore in recent years we seem to be in store for an ongoing litany of this doomed investigation. As Baltimore murders hit 338, the highest per capita rate ever recorded in this sorry city and the highest in this dying nation, Chasing a Killer is a breath of welcome stale air, down to the detail that the murderer used a 1940s revolver, printed in the same issue in which another article claims that Baltimore's handgun problem is the fault of other states not having strict gun laws like Maryland, heralding a call for federal intervention...

'White Racism in Texas'

A Suppressed Story of A Horrific Gang Rape from 2012

© 2015 James LaFond

Tommy's video posts usually get ten times as many views as this. This is a good window on how the blooming race war in the U. S. is virtually being manufactured by the media. Many of my friends will say it is leftist politics, and I may wish to agree. But, do we really have to go any farther than pointing out that fanning race riots pays huge dividends to the media organizations that cause, and then report on, the violence?

This needs to be seen even though it is old news.

11 yo girl Raped by 28 Blk Men In Texas

Just for your information, according to the FBI: for every black woman raped by a white man, 64 white women are raped by black men. The statistics on white male attackers are under dispute because many Latino suspects are listed in police reports as "white," such as Z-Man of Skittle-slaying fame.

https://www.youtube.com/watch?v=TLgWcQCzf0s

Harm City Hoodrats Sweep Urban League

With 344 Kills out of 638 Hits, These Proud Victims of White Privilege Rule the Most Violent City in America

© 2016 James LaFond

In its mania to report on anything but the grim fact that Baltimore is a hunting ground prowled by armed black men—increasingly masked and unchallenged by police—The Baltimore Sun, the journal of record for the Soviet Socialist People's Republic of Maryland, buried the news of December 31st's 8:00 p.m. murder of a young black man in West Baltimore on Popleton Street on the interior page, taking up a thumb's space. The cover stories were on New Year's festivities and increased restrictions on police activity.

Who knows what kind of action there was overnight. Upon my return to Harm City from my night of geriatric debauchery—which now largely consists of snoring in a chair—a half hour ago, at 7 a.m., under a dark dawn sky, I saw a speeding ambulance, two cop cars responding to the area 7-11 with lights on and no sirens. As I sit, the BPD chopper is sweeping the neighborhood from above—one of Baltimore's better neighborhoods...

At a shock trauma surgery cost of $112,000 per target the Home Team is making life flush for area surgeons! Way to take one for the team, Jerome. That vascular surgeon really needed another swimming pool!

More importantly, have these hardworking hoodrats enriched any of the readers at jameslafond.com beyond their mildest dreams?

Below are the murder rate predictions from our Urban League Playoff announcement, the winner to receive a copy of Menthol Rampage.

As you can see, our webmaster, Charles, almost nailed it, which can be expected as he is managing the mapping of habitat hoodrat, checking my unreported violence and aggression against various "murder maps." He is virtually an authority on how to get killed in Baltimore, leaving Steve Lovett, at 345, as our victor.

Charles, send that man a cop of Menthol Rampage!

Steve, if you want a print copy email me at jameslafond.com@gmail.com with your address and I will mail you a copy.

Habibi November 29, 2015 1:20 PM EST

326

Sean November 29, 2015 11:21 AM EST

Wow these guys are worse then I thought. Changing to 335!

Hdob November 22, 2015 12:54 PM EST

317

Charles Meisling November 19, 2015 12:00 PM EST

345

aa November 19, 2015 6:10 AM EST

338

Adam Swinder November 19, 2015 12:03 AM EST

319, go big or go home.

jr November 18, 2015 1:20 PM EST

300,000. We can hope; right?

SAWB November 18, 2015 10:20 AM EST

315, go hoodrats.

Kman November 18, 2015 9:50 AM EST

I'll go with 308. Which coincidentally is my favorite rifle caliber and has never let me down.

K-

Sean November 17, 2015 11:07 AM EST

Can we do over and under bets? If so I'll take the under and if not I'm going for 311.

Ishmael November 17, 2015 11:05 AM EST

328

Don November 17, 2015 12:56 AM EST

Given the pending colder weather I predict the final death count to be 317.

Manny November 16, 2015 11:01 PM EST

I'll take 333. Half the number of the beast. Keep up the good work hood rats!

Sam November 16, 2015 9:36 PM EST

330

Quantrill November 16, 2015 9:35 PM EST

I predict the dindu dance of death slows to a box step with the cool weather... 310.

BIngo November 15, 2015 11:55 PM EST

I'm going to go a bit higher with 336, expecting some hell for the holidays.

Steve Lovett November 15, 2015 7:53 PM EST

345

SidVic November 15, 2015 6:22 PM EST

304

Not the Kitchen
The Place Not To Interview Distraught Psychos

© 2016 James LaFond

In the last week of 2015 six Baltimore County police officers [precinct withheld on request of the officer leaking the information] responded to a home, within which a distraught man was "ranting and raving and screaming."

The man was being talked to in the kitchen when he reached for the butcher block or drawer [it is not clear] and drew a knife, immediately moving on an officer, whereupon he was shot by two or more of the officers and was pronounced dead at the scene.

43

The offices and neighbors were of the opinion that this was "suicide by cop," and, so far as I know, this sad case did not make the news.

My thoughts on this immediately went to the fact that the only place worse than the kitchen to interview a distraught man would be his tool shed. Certainly, when trying to keep a man calm, if he is already in the kitchen, any attempt to remove him might trigger this.

However, for private citizens, never engage in an argument with a person who might become violent in a kitchen. Also, by all means, if someone breaks into your house and you are unarmed, retreat to the kitchen. If the intruder is a hoodrat, might I recommend a palm oil and curry baste...

'Why Should I Avoid Baltimore Campuses?'

'What is So Bad about A City Community College?': A Man Question from Charles

Nationwide community colleges are the focus of black on white mob attacks, almost all of which go unreported by the school or law enforcement and none of which are reported by national media.

These schools are not places where people with money send their kids so that they can party and maybe get a degree. These are schools attended by welfare recipients and the children of welfare recipients, who have no fathers and who are literally just burning time at government expense, so there are a fair variety of impulsive violent crimes, as the entitlement mentality is the root of violence in the domesticated human.

There is also the fact that drug gangs from nearby urban centers or from the urban center in which the open facility is engulfed, will have members embedded in the student body to facilitate drug sales and even to get an education to assist in the operations of the gang.

Then there is the question of that pretty young black girl that you might meet at some mixed race music venue—or even a white venue where she is hunting a white sugar daddy. Most white girls will either go with the gang banger or go with the sugar daddy. Most black girls will do both. In that situation you don't want to be the sugar daddy when Tyrone finds out its not just his pussy.

Copin State, Bowie, College Park, and Morgan State are all notoriously violent Baltimore Area community colleges or state universities that each have a crime rate equal to the ghetto they are in or exceeding that of the surrounding community. The most recent trend in college violence has been revenge stabbings by punks who lost a fight with a jock.

I have been in charge of security details at community colleges and it is a nightmare. The design of these places facilitates aggression in it mob or stalking varieties. They should convert them all to paintball venues.

Stay away from community colleges.

'I'm Confused about Race and Violence'

'Am I Better off Being Black or White When it Comes to Getting Attacked?: A Man Question from Charles

Okay, Charles, out of every 100 acts of violence in the Baltimore Metropolitan Area the acts are initiated at approximately the following rates, though every 100 acts come out slightly different than the next with those I have collected bunching together by happenstance into this pattern:

1 are committed by Latinos*

4 are committed by whites

10 are committed by cop

85 are committed by blacks

Rough guide to source by type, which contradicts the aggression patterns, favoring defenders and witnesses over aggressors:

Latino = 1%

White = 75%

Cops = 2%

Black = 22%

Note that the black population is about 50% in the "Baltimore Area" though higher in the city, with higher percentages of blacks in certain areas always correlating with higher rates of violence.

*The current Latino population is small and unusually docile. This will change.

Of the people I personally know in Baltimore:

Most of the Latinos have been the targets of violence, primarily by blacks

All of the working class whites have been the targets of violence, primarily by blacks, secondarily by cops

Few of the upscale whites have had any experience with violence of any kind, the only ones being those who take part in gentrification initiatives near black ghettos, with people that live in all white suburbs rarely ever experiencing aggression of any type

All of the cops have been targets of violence, primarily by blacks

All of the blacks have had numerous experiences as the targets of violence, primarily by blacks, secondarily by cops

The fact is the Black Baltimore is a predatory matrix and that predators tend to (1) hunt in their home range and (2) select the easiest prey.

So long as blacks are isolated in black ghettos they will almost exclusively prey on one another. When in a mixed environment they will switch to easier white prey. When a white enters the all-black environment, unless he is obviously a predator, he will immediately be slotted as a soft, tasty and eater-friendly morsel.

The important thing to remember is that black predation takes on three forms outside of the dominant gang warfare.

1. Opportunistic predation as soft targets become available is something that roughly one third of the black urban population will engage in impulsively. Drop Donald Trump into a ghetto naked but for his hair and money belt and three out of ten blacks will attack him on sight.

2. Mob attacks are something that five out of ten blacks will engage in if they have been properly incited to lash out at the invisible forces that "keep them down." Wandering into a black area at the wrong time could result in you being mistaken or served up as a scapegoat for these oppressive white forces of evil.

3. About two in ten black males have a highly developed sense of interracial predation and will typically go on lone stalks, paired hunts, or raids with three or more men in the party into predominantly non-black communities. When living, travelling and working outside of a majority black area these are the only types of black attackers you typically need to be concerned with. Note that in black enclaves these types of hunters prey almost exclusively on other blacks. Sometimes the stalker, hunter or raider that is operating in a non-

black area is simply practicing his craft on easy targets, and will eventually return to the ghetto to rob drug dealers. Sometimes he is a specialist and sometimes he has advanced to a more profitable low-risk target base that requires more subtle handling, as police will have an effective presence in most non-black areas.

By avoiding black areas you avoid most mob assaults and a lot of opportunistic aggression.

By avoiding mixed areas you avoid most opportunistic aggression that takes place outside of black enclaves.

Charles, the only reason why black people get attacked more often than white people is that they coexist with other black people at a much higher rate, in closer proximity and for longer periods. Black America has been so perversely sculpted to engage in violence by the sick people that run this nation that the study of violence and aggression in urban and suburban America cannot be undertaken without first acknowledging that race [not interracial relations, but the mere presence or absence of able-bodied blacks] is the primary indicator that acts of violence are likely or imminent.

Habitat Hoodrat: Ho-Nation

When you speak to any black Baltimorean, and have them rate the worst areas to live in, they will rate areas with 100% black occupation as the worst neighborhoods and predominantly white areas as the most desirable.

'My Baby'

Hoodrat Feeding Frenzy on Combat Incubator: Tommy Sotomayor's New Years BT-1000 Post

© 2016 James LaFond

8 Black Beasties Jump 1 Pregnant Beast While SIMP Records & Commentates The Whole Thing

Checkout the dominant Silver Back Bitch hammering the combat incubator. The males are passive. The old silver back with the cane does attempt a feeble rescue.

You White Nationalists fear blacks?

Are you kidding me?

American blacks—all of them—could not win a war against one company of Kurdish combat incubators, let alone men.

What you need to fear is the media-Police state that is sponsoring and protecting these hoodrats, and who will come after you after you defend yourself. Hoodrats are just the joker in the State Poker hand.

Look at this video, at what you fear:

By the way, this is about how black men fight these days, just like those who taught them. The only thing to fear is the cowardice of the rest of America and the counter-attack by the pigs.

Oh yes, black lives matter.

Note that one woman pushes on the fetus.

One man could have ended this—but, other men would have attacked him as he violated their goddess.

https://www.youtube.com/watch?v=MVHr-GzhLpU&feature=em-subs_digest

'The Power of A General-Father'

Monster: The Autobiography of an L.A. Gang Member by Sanyika Shakur, aka Monster Kody Scott

© 2016 James LaFond

1991, Penguin, NY, 383 pages

The title says it all, fatherless boys looking for a reason to rise and an excuse to rebel against what they intuitively know is a sick, materialistic society. If I were a young black man this would be my life, killing other degenerates and trying to outsmart a system so big and dumb it's immune to subterfuge.

Kody was a well-off welfare kid in 1974 [more well-off than I was being born in the same year, with two parents working], with the best schooling taxes could pay for, excellent clothes, the latest sneakers, and a yearning for something masculine, something other than his mother could give him. The proof that he never escaped her vagina is in the dedication, "To my dear mother, Birdie M. Scott, who had the courage to push me out in a world of which we control so little."

Only in an emasculated, materialistic society can a man who has been in gunfights in L.A. and knife fights in Folsom, and who has been shot 7 times, truly believe that a bitch laying an egg and collecting a minimum wage salary for the kid as it raises itself, constitutes heroism.

Kody Scott and I were born in the same year, and if he is alive, we are enemies. But I like his viewpoint; his insistence that he is a soldier of the New Afrikans, that he is forever at war with the white Americans and brown Chicanos. I might see him as my enemy, and he might see me as his enemy, but both see the same evil puppet master pulling his strings above it all.

I liked Kody's story, his refusal to let go of his militant, adolescent construct, which, for all of its affectations is more authentic than what my parents believed in. He has wisdom of a sort, will never understand how he became a disposable tool for something too big for his shallow mind to grasp, but soldiers on in his mind's eye with a wisdom appropriate to his perspective, "Prison loomed in my future like wisdom teeth; if you lived long enough you got them. Prison was like a stepping stone to manhood."

At the end of his book, hopefully just to please his editors or his 'indomitable" wife, Kody decries the notion that he and the other gang bangers from South Central L.A. destroyed their own neighborhood in the Rodney King Riots any more than the Vietnamese destroyed their own country attacking U.S. firebases. He is against multi-culturalism, and unfortunately regrets the good deeds he did in life, such as killing gangsters, but his heart is in the right place: sour, unfulfilled, lied to and restless despite his age. What I like the most about his story is how he explains his entry into "gangsterism," by being surprised and betrayed in a "jump in" attack arranged by older boys, which is the same way most gangsters exit the gang life, by taking a bullet in the back of the head from a friend, and he nearly admits it, beating so far around that traitorous bush as to prune it to the trunk.

I like Kody Scott, see him as a worthy foe, and if he is alive, we should arrange a death match. It would make more sense than the next presidential election.

Kody should speak for himself here:

"We cannot contaminate them [our children] with our feuds of madness, which are predicated on factors over which we have no control."

'Mamma, Wait!'
An Exceptionally Well-Equipped Shoplifting Attempt

© 2016 James LaFond

As I was heading down to the local ghetto grocer for my milk, crossing the parcel pickup area, a very, very large black woman was pushing a cart of groceries out into the Sunday afternoon air. She was about five feet ten inches and perhaps 450 pounds, with breasts the size of an NFL helmet, dressed in stretchy tiger-stripe pants and shirt, with a purple ruffled vest and knee high vinyl hooker boots.

Behind her came the Nigerian security guard shouting, "Mamma, Mamma, wait. Stop, Mamma, I must have what is in your shirt!"

The woman stopped, turned like a tigress at bay and snarled menacingly at the 160 pound middle-aged man, who skipped forward on tip toe like he was trying to reach his hand into a tank of swarming hornets. Like a veritable Mowgli he deftly inserted his hand into the gargantuan cleavage before the creature could engulf him in her beastly embrace and withdrew a two pound box of frozen hamburger patties from between the woman's breasts!

As she scowled, and he skipped away sprite-like with joy, said, "Have a nice day, Mamma, come again."

Meanwhile, Mister Lee, the hacker on duty, said, "Good Lord, ain't nobody want to buy them funky burgers now!"

18 Steps Into Hell
Reading Houses: Assessing Residential Areas to Determine Aggression Patterns

© 2016 James LaFond

Have you seen the "decorative" barred storm doors on the fronts of homes?

These are not just decorative. Practically speaking you cannot kick them in, so they do provide summertime security for people concerned with street crime who want to be able to look out at their children playing and to check on a parked car while securely behind bars. Security experts will tell you that these are not secure doors, and they are not. They are, however, 90% more secure than a normal storm door.

But even this does not matter. All that matters is that the person buying it does so to feel secure.

Habitat Hoodrat: Ho-Nation

You are looking at houses in order for the homeowner to tell you what he or she thinks about their neighborhood and the people that walk through it. Primarily, what decoratively barred storm doors indicate, is that the homeowners fear the people who walk through their neighborhood.

Below is a graduated list of home owner warnings that you are entering a predation zone. In all cases the more of this you see the worse. Note that bars only go on windows after the property has been broken into.

1. Property is not being maintained

2. For sale sign

3. Decorative, barred storm door

4. Barred or blocked back basement window

5. Property is damaged and unrepaired

6. Barred or blocked windows at ground level on side of house [usually on corner houses]

7. No ground-level window air conditioners in summer

8. A wrought iron or stainless steel cage or fence around porch or yard, usually on corner houses near bus stops

9. Foreclosure signs

10. Vacant house

11. Gutted, vacant house

12. Gutted, vacant house, in front of which residents [and non-residents] congregate as if it is a concrete community park

13. Bars in second story windows above roofed porches, which means that some hoodrat has climbed onto the roof of a porch and entered through an upstairs window on the street front! These are regular features in some Harm City neighborhoods.

14. Barbed or razor wire on top of fences, fenced and caged fire escapes and balconies on the side and rear.

15. Fortified parking pad [Yes, we found one in Baltimore City], basically a Bat Cave or A-Team Headquarters

16. Blocked out windows and doors in a still occupied house

17. Stamped steel security doors and stamped steel enclosed windows

18. Teams of men stationed on porches visited by boys who do not stick around

Note: 16-18 are indications of an ongoing criminal operation at that location—and they are afraid of the dudes on the street, because police only stop by here to pick up bodies, not kick in doors.

The best indication of home invasion-level threats can be had by examining corner row homes where there is an alley or access road behind the row.

Big Trippin's Snow Shovel
A Winter Tale of A Baltimore Expatriate

© 2016 James LaFond

From a meeting in the driveway of a house with a reader who has moved away from Baltimore after experiencing its worst.

The menace, intimidation and threat you describe in your [Harm City] writing is so alive in my mind after living in Baltimore. We actually lived on North Avenue at the base of [redacted] Hill, next to some drug dealer. I don't even want to get into any details because we still know people down there.

Up here it is so totally a different environment. It was almost a shocking experience, not to have to measure your step, narrow your eyes and run scenarios through your mind just going from Point A to Point B.

We do have our urban elements, somehow regurgitated out here by the Powers That Be, who just seem determined to seed every corner of the land with criminal elements.

I had not lived up here for long and made the cardinal sin of leaving my snow shovel on the porch after shoveling.

[Laughter]

You know in Baltimore that thing is gone in minutes. Of course I'm conditioned to the urban environment and step outside to check on the shovel, and sure enough some Dominican kid is walking off with it!

Before I can even do anything this really big Dominican man yells at this kid—

thunders at him with anger—"Put it back! What the hell are you doing? Don't you know this is why they hate us!"

And the kid brings the shovel back. So it's not exactly like Baltimore—not even a little, really...[where you would have had a man supervising and supporting the theft, or a mother ordering it.]

I could tell that this man had come out here for a similar reason, to get away from the crime. It was a very interesting thing.

-Big Trippin

For more on Big Trippin's experiences see also *Big Trippin's Myerhoff Mugging*

"My Eyes Can't See Around Corners"

Bicyclist's Lives Don't Matter: With Advice from Onetime Harm City Cyclist Nero the Pict

http://stuffblackpeopledontlike.blogspot.com/2016/01/third-black-suspect-arrested-in.html

"Being around drug dealers is safer for Neanderthal descendants than the sons of middle class community activists! Bicycles are literally worse than being on foot it seems with these attacks..."

"What do you know about Waverly?"

-Mescaline

Waverly?

My Uncle Bill and his three sons grew up in Waverly.

It was a race war zone 40 years ago.

30 years ago Rick's son had his nose bitten clean off in a fight with another white dude there.

Mixed race area on the bus line to Mondawmin, with a major transfer point right there.

Close to the Hopkins campus, upscale Charles Village and Union Memorial hospital. A doctor who worked emergency room there had one black mugger come in with two slashed wrists, two slashed hamstrings, and a stab to the kidney which just pierced fat. He had tried to rob a small Latino/Asian guy. He admitted to trying to rob the smaller man, who was all of a sudden behind him.

Currently muggings, bump-and-stop carjacking, rapes, recreational mob stompings.

The Story

I have been spending a lot of time moving round Baltimore City by car looking at residential neighborhoods, and can tell you that for sale signs are averaging 2 out of every 10 houses. A lot of people cannot get out except as a refugee. Many middle-aged people whose houses lost value seven years ago are actually fortifying their houses.

The victim in this attack looks, forgive me, like a ready made target. Nice white guys die in Baltimore. Mass transit is just as unsafe. Unless you can afford a car in Baltimore you are a hunted animal. Most people just do not have the skill set to deal with this type of predation.

To deal with this type of attack you must use a knife from a concealed hand position—do not brandish it—grab one shirt and stab under the heart, rip down and in, in a reverse C cut and then get another one. If you do not gut two you will do serious time. If you only cut/stab one, the rest are all witnesses. Cut and stab as many as possible.

Insane Welfare Whore Alliance
Hood-Rat Hatching Mud Sharks Spawning the Next Thug Generation

© 2016 James LaFond

This week, as food stamps peak and a blizzard is predicted for Central Maryland, it has been a tough day at the office for the Ghetto Grocer. Just after midnight a new EBT group came in, immensely fat military age white men riding in handy capped carts spending government EBT disbursements, black drug dealers and their snow bunnies, white dope fiends and zombie crack whores, malformed mud sharks with their little brown babies, wearing pajamas and dirty socks, insane white spinsters buying cat food, cat litter, cat toys and organic gluten free food…

There was one intact family unit, and they were a black teenage couple of perhaps 16, with their two-year old baby, both of them already dropped out of school, her on welfare, him doing whatever he does to afford the two-wheeled standup device he is driving his toddler around on, as she stands between his feet on the platform, pressing her little hands to the inside of his knees as he zooms by me while I kneel in front of the sour cream case cleaning the vents...

This morning an upscale set of white parasites, fifty-year-old government retirees, discussing their vacations, homes, automobiles and children's college tuition paid for by grunts like me, chatted about their good fortune while I stocked yogurt. It no longer hurts though, for I have pared down my earnings so far that the only taxes I pay is the $1,000 annual fine for not having free health care.

In all of this insanity over the past 24 hours I have only recorded two acts of aggression, and these acts were, as usual, perpetrated by the most entitled class of people in our society, black women and unemployed white women, who aspire to the heights of ebony womanhood in all of its glory, though they don't carry that foodstamp induced weight gain as well and their little lottery tickets are not of the rich chocolate hue they would prefer.

Two white welfare skanks, who seemed to be in their early twenties, though they had forty-year-old faces, and seemed to have been designed by God to carry between 100-120 pounds on their frames, which were now saddled with about 350 pounds each, began cussing out Steevo in the aisle for being in their way. They had already threatened a deli person for not being able to magically generate sliced cheese that comes out to exactly two dollars, not cutting her the slack for not being able to calculate the weight of a slice of cheese [which varies from type to type], that they had cut themselves, by demanding an exact dollar amount for their cheese purchase, rather than asking for a pound or fraction thereof.

I was in the stockroom, next to the woman's room [the only space available] unloading a pallet of freight, when Betty and Steevo came back to cool off, and gripe, as us lowly peasants may not speak up to our masters and mistresses, who live freely upon our labor.

Steevo moaned, "I can't even afford a pizza for the wife and kid on Friday night, and these fat whores have a thousand dollars on their EBT card just for spreading their legs and laying fucking milkdud eggs. I had to come back here. I can't have some whore screaming at me for doing my job. I mean, back in the day, getting beat up by the pigs, having them use the phone book on you, I got that. Sure, they were dicks. But I was a dick too for selling dope and running from them. But this, having to be the slave to some fat hog who is buying her shit with my taxes dollars, fuck that! Doesn't it bother you, Bro?"

"No, man. I think its great. I live down in the city where the thugs that were spawned by three generations of welfare whores try to rob me or whack me any chance they get. Now, thanks to Mamma Mud Shark, when you're my age, her three whigger babies will be coming for you in their hoodies and fitted hats! Welcome to the ghetto, Bro—we deliver!"

Steevo walked away in even more pain, having been ministered to by a Doctor of the Retail Food Arts. Betty just rolled her eyes and peeled off with him.

Then, as I hit the orange juice at the bottom of the pallet and put on my gut brace, Karma, in the form of Mamma Mud Shark, whose pudendum had a double chin and her face a triple, waddled back to the woman's room—the door of which does not shut properly, much to my disgust—and I began heaving 32-pound cases as fast as my splitting gut would allow. Sure enough, within minutes, as I hit wood and tilted the pallet up to push it to the dock, I heard her scream/growl from her fetid seat, "You cheap muvafuckers! What is this, packing paper? Get me some muvafuckin' Charmin!"

I all of a sudden remembered I had to check the drains under the frozen food cases and veered off into the peasant's first and last refuge, work.

Later this morning, Monique, a French-speaking Spanish babe, who I once won over with the following line, "I don't always work in supermarkets, but when I do, I work here," came to me breathless, excited about a close call on the street driving to the local ghetto grocer for her morning yogurt and banana before heading off to work in White Breadistan. Since becoming a jameslafond.com reader, Monique has become a big Tommy Sotomayor fan, which should help you understand the following.

"You would have been proud of me, Mister Violence Guy! I was about to turn down Eastern Avenue off the highway when I noticed it was hazardous. Then, from behind me this BT-one-thousand, in her giant SUV, began beeping at me and telling me to go. I have always thought that was my decision to make. But apparently not, so I flipped her off. Then I noticed her pulling up beside me and saw how big she was, and thought, wow, that may be a BT-twelve-hundred, and I zoomed out of there."

"Was it a silverback?"

"I really couldn't tell. The SUV was so big it might have skewed my sense of proportions."

"Look, I don't know what you're driving, but if you don't date a drug dealer it's probably not an Escalade or a Tahoe. I guarantee you that a silver back BT-one-thousand—even an eight-hundred—could get right through the window. You should not flip off a Black Terminatrix. Remember, it does not feel pity or remorse, and will not stop, ever!"

She smiled and made off with her groceries waving, "Thank you!"

This all was kind of fun as conversations go, but Steevo, Patty and Monique were all noticeably upset after their run-ins with aggressively entitled females, parasites of the most vile sort, deliberately generated by our masters, to drain us of our dignity and resolve, and to spawn the next generation of violent criminals, who shall cause us to beg our masters for more laws, and more police to enforce them, because the police we have are there to protect the criminals from us, so that we have to take it.

Yes, my police chopper is back, kind of late. It's already 11:21 a.m. the local thugs must have hit the malt liquor hard last night. The first robbery is usually about 11 on the dot.

The Insane Welfare Whore Alliance does not exist just to support drug dealers. In fact, their primary purpose is to erode the moral fabric of human society by producing criminals to justify the growth of the Police State, the State that in reality polices us more effectively than them.

Let the next bitch-egg hatch, so that we might beg for a new, improved morality.

Beware Unknown Suspects!
Do These Phantom Gunmen and Knifers Come from Regal, Sirus, Alpha Centuri, Cetu or Planet Hood Rat!

© 2016 James LaFond

In the two areas of Baltimore County I frequent we get more crime coverage than in all of Baltimore City, from small local papers, albeit owned by the big one, which is owned either by Baalzeebub or Lucifer, I think, or is it Hades?

Although there are no crimes in Baltimore City other than murders, according to our Mayor and the journal of record, kicking in front doors is becoming very popular among thugs in outlying areas. It is, however, difficult to track these people down—assuming they are people—as the police have apparently been unable to discover anything about the violent felons in Parkville, Essex and Dundalk.

On Tuesday, January 12, a "victim" was robbed by two presumably unarmed "suspects" on U.S. Route #1.

Friday, January 15, about midnight, in Parkville, on Waltham Woods, "two victims" were robbed at gunpoint by "two unknown suspects."

Meanwhile, over on the East Side, at one minute after midnight, in Middle River, at the Martin Blvd. shopping center [probably at the #4 bus stop] a "victim" of undetermined genus, species [considering the weather, probably a mammal], race or sex, was robbed at knife point by "two unknown suspects" [presumably earthlings], presumably higher primates with opposable thumbs.

Back on the 9th, at a Taco Bel, not far from where our first "victim" of undetermined type, some idiot got out of his buddy's truck to have words with someone giving them a hard time in the drive thru behind them, could not see through the tinted windows, and walked over to the driver's side to peer into the car through the conveniently open window and was shot.

Oh yes, and down in Dundalk some poor bastard was run over and left dead in the street, the nature of his attacker having the virtue of being an authentic mystery.

These reports serve no purpose other than to identify hot spots. We do not have any ability to inform the police as we are woefully uninformed.

We do not know if Raccoons are organizing, perhaps mounted on the backs of vengeful whitetail deer and hunting humans, or if these are actually humans doing this, let alone one kind of human.

Furthermore—assuming these are humans—we do not know what kind of people are being hunted. Are the people of my age, race, gender being attacked?

If so, by what type of attacker?

There is only one rational explanation, that these victims are from one group of people that the authorities [including the media] do not want to inform as to their peril, lest they become vigilant, or perhaps move, and the unknown suspects are all members of a protected group that the authorities do not want to be suspected of doing what they do. Aside from these vague assumptions, we can only determine one thing for certain, that the police and the media, want whoever is being attacked to continue being attacked and whoever is attacking to continue attacking under the cloak of anonymity.

They do not even need to wear hoods.

'Chill Out'
No, Don't, Beat Her Man into A Pulp!

© 2016 James LaFond

Black S I M P Gets PoundCaked Over His Black Girlfriend Running Her Mouth To A Thug!

I have to disagree with Tommy on this. I think the man-child with the "big-old ape woman" deserved what he was served. Sorry Tommy, but as far as this Neanderthal is concerned, black-on-black crime is just fine.

For non-Nubians, who think that they will be able to defend themselves against a man who has a black video-conscious woman with him, without suffering the force of law, look at how this bitch stage-managed this entire thing. They will get you arrested, will get you into court, because they have worked this sick system of ours so thoroughly that they believe they own it, and they might be getting closer to right on that count.

https://www.youtube.com/watch?v=R-fI_nzJK-o&feature=em-subs_digest

Spreading the Love
Harm City Update: 2/3/16

I have been spending most of my time indoors, leading the life of a literary hermit, doing solo training at the gym, dedicating little of my time to researching the crimescape of Baltimore, other than in mapping the town block-by-block, as a public service, an effort that seems to be three weeks from release in this first edition.

From speaking with people who are on foot more than I am, and checking in the smaller community news papers, we are looking at a focus in the City itself on property crime, due to the decreased mobility of police during the blizzard and the pathetic half-assed clean-up, that is still not complete nearly two weeks on, with warm weather for half of those days. The fact that hoodrats are not, apparently, all-terrain bipeds, but pure pavement crawlers, has cut down markedly on beatings and muggings in the city, with no mob attacks I know of over the past two weeks. Part of this is due to schools being closed for a week.

In Harm County, however, the Baltimore City Housing Authority initiative to buy houses and pay for rental space in outlying municipalities is paying off. Shootings in the Essex precinct are up. Home owners and renters are fleeing Essex faster than any other county precinct. Armed robberies and home invasions are up across Eastern Baltimore County, although they are being reported as simple assaults and burglaries. Essex was fairly well been abandoned by the police at night, ever since the April 2015 race purge, during which not one single Baltimore County officer was seen on patrol by myself or anyone I spoke with for a full week, as gangs of armed black men prowled main streets and beat lone white men with impunity—none of which was reported through hospital channels or in the papers, even the local papers—as resources are diverted to Towson. In fact, my son is now moving from Essex to Towson, in part, for this reason.

Eastern Baltimore County is being abandoned by county police even as:

1. Resources are diverted to the Towson City Line

2. Record numbers of Baltimore City welfare families are being resettled in Eastern Baltimore County [the Dundalk, Essex, White Marsh, Parkville precincts]

3. Actual violence has doubled or tripled in Eastern Baltimore County and stayed static in Towson [the County Seat].

4. Violence is not decreasing in Baltimore City, other than the winter weather event

5. Police in Baltimore City respond to 911 calls at less than half the frequency, do not check 311 calls until days later, and are observing no-go zones where no violence that does not produce a body is reported.

6. A 20-agent Federal task force is helping with major crimes.

7. Baltimore County is forgiving the roughly quarter-million dollar debt of Baltimore City for help during the riots.

8. BPD tactical caravans—ten to 15 vehicles deep, with marked cop cars front and back, unmarked cars in the front and tactical vehicles in the center—are striking into west Baltimore daily between 3:30 and 5:00 a.m.

9. The DOJ is pressuring municipal police departments to get rid of their tactical vehicles, which were the only units of the BPD who were able to stand up—let alone go after—the teenagers that rioted in April/ of 2015.

10. According to the motorists I speak to, traffic stops have increased in frequency three-fold since mid 2015, in the County, but not in the City, where they remain the same.

I leave the reader to draw their own conclusions.

Ground Ho Day?
Harm City Hoodrats Honor a Rural Tradition

As the perennially beleaguered, girthy rodent of Pennsylvania fame was once again dragged from its cozy winter burrow by superstitious bipeds to determine if winter would indeed come to an end, sooner rather than later, his urban cousins took seasonal forecasting into their own hands here, in Harm City, south of Yo Adrian's Wall...

Migrant hoodrats have continued to shoot each other and local wannabe hoodrats in the outlying areas of Eastern Baltimore County at a rate not seen since the 1990s at the height of the drug wars.

Habitat Hoodrat: Ho-Nation

Hoodrats, lone ones, and paired scouting parties, have been seen with increasing frequency up to 10 miles beyond the Baltimore City line, scouting the middle class residential neighborhoods to which they have been relocated by the Master of Hoodrats in his dark tower—it's white? Are you sure, Charles?

A man leaving a night club was attacked and robbed on the parking lot by two hoodrats, six miles from the city line.

Ten miles from Harm City a mated pair of hoodrats attacked a woman in the Carroll Island Walmart, two miles from waterfront mansions. The male hoodrat applied a rear standing choke while the female hoodrat attempted—unsuccessfully—to take a ring from a finger, and did take the victim's purse, which was later recovered.

Since the snow cleared, numerous individual Neanderthals have been attacked and robbed in White Marsh, Essex, Rosedale and Parkville, by packs of warm-weather acclimated hoodrats. Didn't this happen when the snow cleared for the spring 30,000 years ago?

The kicking in of front doors and basement doors is now the most common aspect of property crime in the above mentioned areas. All such reports have been limited to print and online media, with no [according to my TV-viewing sources] TV coverage of this trend.

And, putting aside the two stabbings and assorted gunpoint robberies, the true sign that hoodrat summer is here, is that, on Thursday, January 28th, as soon as the snow had cleared enough to make hoodrat mobility practical, at 2:40 in the afternoon, at the BP gas station on Compass Road, in upscale White Marsh, two "unknown suspects," [possibly Alpha Centurian infiltrators, but most likely Harm City hoodrats], threatened the victim [also unknown, but assumed to be a Neanderthal] with a hand gun, demanding his clothes. The two "unknown suspects" then took the victim's clothes and fled. Had they been dispatched by a hoodrat matriarch to acquire bedding for her den, or perhaps clothing for her "mans?"

This is an important detail. If the Neanderthal was fleeced for bedding then we have six more weeks of winter, if for the stately appearance of Mamma's mans at the Golden Buffet, then summer is as good as here.

This reporter suspects that summer is as good as here!

Tres Hombres
Harm City Hoodrats facing Competition From Feral Fat Heads

© 2016 James LaFond

Last weekend, just around the corner from my young friend Andrew's well-appointed cardboard box [actually a pyramid of 4 waxed cardboard pumpkin/watermelon bins wired together] the local liquor store in this outlying area of East Baltimore, was entered by three cagey "Latinos."

The next day the three fat heads returned and robbed the proprietor. On was armed with a handgun, another with a machete, and another was unarmed. This is an excellent method for detailing responsibility, which is generally quite beyond the organizational capacity of the Harm City Hoodrat.

94

Habitat Hoodrat: Ho-Nation

I see this incident as a positive sign for Harm City. Any ecosystem that has only two predators [pigs and hoodrats] competing for prey will tend to stagnate along a polar axis. Not only do I see the Harm City watering hole to be a more balanced food chain, if this trend continues, but also look forward to the day when Feral Fat Heads eradicate the Harm City Hoodrat.

'Villainy Reigns'
Hunting Whitey in Philadelphia

© 2016 James LaFond

Two Years After Blacks Killed Amber Long Over a $14 Purse, Philadelphia Detectives Have No Leads in Solving Her Murder

Amber

http://stuffblackpeopledontlike.blogspot.com/2016/02/two-years-after-blacks-killed-amber.html

"Interesting security video, it was quick but they scouted with the car before."

-Dominick

Thanks for the heads up Dom.

This blogger does work hard and brings valuable reality to our attention, but is so painfully naïve as to boggle the mind. Please let us leave justice, decency and notions of wrong out of the discussion of state-facilitated predation by 80-IQ bipeds.

Notice the use of the hooded sweat shirts, garb of the innocent, a garment that could not have been better designed to facilitate such crimes.

Of course women are not tactically-minded, and there is no possibility that they could have resisted these two mugs even if there was no gun. The only possibility was them having guns and being alert, and we cannot have armed prey in Habitat Hoodrat. However, if this were two Neanderthal males, you would want to stack in echelon, which is an offset pattern, left hand of follow-on man in line to touch right shoulder of lead man. The rear man has the knife, and he taps when he is about to make his stab. Unarmed parties should concentrate on pinning the hand in the right pocket.

The hoody is defeated by checking the right hand in the pocket with your left and then either stabbing the ape in the neck, or grabbing the hood and pulling it over his head with the right hand—keep puling until it is hung up inside-out on his wrists.

Homicide 915 North Front St DC# 14 26-002713

https://www.youtube.com/watch?v=pYfIYVI3ilU

Year of the Monkey in the NBA?
Chinese Insult Liberal American Chattel

© 2016 James LaFond

http://www.dailymail.co.uk/news/article-3428508/Sacramento-Kings-nix-racially-insensitive-Chinese-New-Year-Monkey-T-shirt-giveaway-day-Black-History-Month.html

"Conflicting multicultural streams. Steve Sailer is like the Year of the Monkey has been going on since 206 BC."

-Mescaline Franklin

Okay, Mescaline, thanks, but no thanks. I have to spar today and I think I just lost my left-nut laughing over this story, so please, next time, how about a warning that I could endanger myself via reading the link...

And yes, I am insulted too—my fellow Harm Citizens are not monkeys, they are great apes, crossbred by Big-Headed Yakub with the Norway rat and the neutrino to serve as an urban buffer force against the ineradicable white devils he accidentally bred in the laboratory caves of Patmos!

Bring Us Your Curious, Your Young, Your Weak

Harm County North Buckles Under Harm City Pressure

© 2016 James LaFond

Harm County North, known to the indigenous rednecks and the urban cowards that fled there from their ebony masters a generation ago, as Harford County, has been targeted by urban planners, real estate moguls and politicians for ghettoization. With crime on the rise in Harford County due to the Baltimore Housing Authority buying houses outside of its jurisdiction and settling hoodrats there, and with every urban flight transplant knowing of someone who was recently attacked in Baltimore while attempting to get back and forth to work or to an entertainment venue, semi-privileged brows have been raised to the point of—oh, no—reason. No, we cannot have that!

Although the actual crime occurring in Baltimore is either being ignored by police, under reported or reclassified, social media keeps people informed as to the actuality to enough of an extent to enable the application of some common sense.

In a rare bid for sanity, the Harford County School District had cancelled all field trips for students into Baltimore, as it is clearly an unsafe environment. The mulattress mayor [the same whore who let the city burn and then requested that 1,000 Somali refugees be settled in Baltimore] was outraged. Phone calls were made, and the school authorities waffled, and will now be sending their children into harm's way, where else, but in Harm City.

How bad is Baltimore, during the day, on Baltimore Street, three blocks from the largest police precinct of the eighth largest police department in the nation?

Once, at 4 p.m. an innocent, unarmed, oppressed individual attempted to hold up a Secret Service agent at gunpoint—oops!

A county executive from a surrounding municipality sat in his car, stuck in traffic with his wife, as a mob of innocent, unarmed, oppressed youth rampaged down the street with bats.

On the Corner of Light and Baltimore, Timmy was attacked by two men at a busy bus stop at 8:30 a.m. during rush hour. The bus driver did not blink, did not even call the police.

At 11:00 a.m. one morning I had an innocent, unarmed, oppressed individual threaten me like so, "I'll kill yo ass, Yo," for no apparent reason.

Way back in the day, when I was 13 year's old, walking down Light Street with my father, a man tried to walk me into an alley, by coming up next to me and putting his arm around me. My father shoved him off and walked me out of there, and that was a decade before crack hit the streets.

I have an idea, if the Harford County School District would like to schedule a field trip, I will be willing to conduct a tour of Habitat Hoodrat, gratis. All I want is a set of binoculars, a riding crop, kaki shorts, and a pith helmet for my trouble. I'll even show your brats how to get served at a Korean liquor store—two of them did survive the purge, you know!

Below is the link to a news story on the subject. "Indefinitely" is apparently a fleeting notion in Harford County, as the decision was reversed almost immediately.

http://baltimore.cbslocal.com/2016/02/08/harford-co-putting-school-trips-to-baltimore-city-on-hold-indefinitely/

Walking in the Street
Why Certain People Walk in the Street Instead of on the Sidewalk

"As someone who seems to understand the mysterious behaviors of those urban Americans who move out from the city and into suburbia, perhaps you could explain to me why certain people walk in the street instead of on the sidewalk. Is this an attempt to win a lawsuit? Why risk your life in the street when you could safely walk on the sidewalk?"

-Nelson

Thanks, Nelson. I was feeling under the weather today, and you have reignited my ravenous intellect with a question for the ages. So, play deep, brother, because I'm about to hit this one out of the ballpark...

First, Nelson, recall, that as with any other laboratory animal subject to artificially induced stresses, the American Hoodrat, is a highly conditioned creature, a virtual creation of the oligarchic, federal mind.

I might as well ask you, Mister Nelson, of Whitebreadistan, why, if in Kebmo and WrayWray's neighborhood, your white ass would insist on walking the narrow gauntlet of ambuscades, muggings and mob stompings that is the urban sidewalk, when you could walk down the middle of the unused street?

You see, Kebmo and WrayWray have a set of neighbors who are violent, opportunistic predators living in their dens on side streets never patrolled by the police, making their sidewalks quite dangerous. Also, since not enough stupid white people have come into their neighborhood to enable them to earn enough cash "jacking fools up in front a da stoop," these violent people have not been able to purchase an automobile.

The people that do drive are responsible elements of society like, the dummy that works, the drug dealer, the pimp, the hitter, and the stripper, who would not run someone over in the street. White people, especially, are averse to squashing hood rats under their tires, and the hood rats know this, trusting the white people driving through their newly subsidized environs to avoid striking them with their car, but still leery of sidewalks, because they know, that the first predatory hoodrat who claims this street as his hunting ground, is going to begin hitting targets on the sidewalks, not in the street.

Class Dismissed.

Women and Strangers
Stranger Aggressions against Women in Baltimore, MD, January 2015 through February 2016

© 2016 James LaFond

This is a reference for a friend of mine who is a karate instructor and is beginning a women's self defense course. The following is a list from most to least common of stranger aggression against women in Baltimore that I've documented over the past 14 months. All of the following aggressions, except for the flash mob attack and the carjacking, take place at night exclusively.

1. Most common are strong-arm robberies at her place of employment, usually at a 7-11, farm store, ice cream shop, or fast food joint, all committed by adult black males. Of these highly vulnerable cash-handling positions, the safest job—-the cash

register operating woman least likely to be robbed—-is the barmaid.

2. Strong-arm robbery of a lone woman entering or exiting her vehicle. This has been done by black youths, singly and in pairs, and lone adult black males. Vehicle approach and egress is a major tactical concern of women who do not wish to be victimized.

3. A handgun robbery committed in the same work environments as described in item one. This crime has only been committed by adult males, both black and white.

4. A handgun robbery committed in the same circumstances described in item two. This has only been committed by lone adult black males.

5. The woman and her male date are targeted for robbery at night on a sidewalk or parking lot by a pair of men, one of whom is armed with a handgun. The woman may be robbed, but she is not the target. The man has been targeted because he is with the woman and therefore has limited defensive options. This is because the dynamic here is that women cannot outrun young men, so the male date loses his most survivable option against a handgun threat which is to run away. This is always perpetrated by groups of black youth or

adult black males, usually in pairs but sometimes trios.

6. A bump and stop carjacking in which two or three men stage a minor collision and then take the vehicle when the woman exits to exchange information. This has happened on the busiest primary streets of Baltimore during rush hour. Only black males—- ages vary, but most of these are in their 20s.

7. A flash mob attack in which a woman and a friend, male or female, are targeted for recreational violence by three to 50 black teenagers, predominantly from the middle class.

8. Threat or challenge to fight by a black woman in a parking lot, or at retail or dining establishments, motivated by rage-based aggression. The single best solution for this is not to verbally engage the threatening party.

9. Forced entry into home through front door, sometimes posing as a sales/service call or by just breaking in the door, all perpetrated by black males, who primarily take the car keys from the resident and then take the car parked out front.

10. Knife-point rape by either lone black youth or a group of black youth. This is a dominance crime,

and the attackers have expressed a willingness to stab a woman if she fights or screams. These attackers have not persisted when interrupted by a male.

11. Strong-arm rape/gang rape by drunken Hispanic laborers, possibly just a sex crime performed through the use of force.

The Hoodrat Trace
Counter-Hunting the Urban Savage

© 2016 James LaFond

On the Old Frontier, the frontier of Simon Kenton, Daniel Boone and Lewis Wetzel, wilderness men did not follow paths or trails, but traces, a mental image of a wilderness route through which one would pick his way, many of which later became "trails" and roads.

Here, in Harm City, in my own Indian Country, I also do not blaze a trail or follow a set route, but pick my way. Yesterday, as I headed down to the market to purchase my tea bags, I was unarmed, something I no longer risk at night, but a chance I willingly take when I know I shall be hunted by the oppressed minions of the State in their innocent meekness. I left the old plantation house at 2 p.m., knowing full well that I would have to navigate through throngs and knots of violent middle school and high school students, most larger than I, few likely to be combat-effective. If I were to defend against any of these with a pocket knife my name would be mud, everything with my name on it taken out of publication, etc.

I will not, however, fight a mob of hoodrats with my bare hands. On the way down, I took note of a rusty iron shank in the gutter on my street. A little further along was a lifted chunk of curb, heavy enough to crush a foot. As I turned the corner onto Harford Road, I passed the crumbling stone wall with hand axe-shaped rocks for the picking. Fifty yards down is the Big Bad Wolf eatery, where a five pound half block is used to keep the lid from blowing off of their trash can. Further down, in front of the Pakistani pizzeria, where drugs are dealt openly, a pointed, fist-size stone lays at the base of the poorly growing decorative pear tree.

On my way back, a single-use 24 ounce glass bottle in my hand, prepped to smash hoodrat craniums, I notice thirty to forty hoodrats on the left side, and only three knots of five to seven on the right side, so took the right side. As I pass each group, careful not to swerve out of their way, but shoulder through, less I be marked as easy prey, I recall where each stone is, and where the "back-to-the-wall" defensive position is, where I intend to shuffle to if attacked.

A group of wannabe, middleclass thugs spot me and spread out, one of them puffing out his chest and hooting at me to frighten the old man—who walks directly for him, intent on barreling through to the doorway to make his stand. The knot tightens up defensively and I straighten my course towards the three older, posing, mixed-race thugs walking toward me 20 yards past these twerps. These older teens spread out to shoulder me into the gutter.

I switch the grip on the bottle for a stab to the gut, and keep my eye on the pizzeria stone in the planter behind them. The flanker on my side gives ground and packs up with the others, and I continue on by.

After a time, I look over my shoulder and see a 40-year-old black cruiserweight carrying his groceries, and using the same edging tactics, herding the lesser primates into easily smashed bunches as they give ground and he rolls his shoulders menacingly.

We make eye-contact as I turn and he follows me down the street where he also lives. I do not know this man, but have walked with him in snow, rain, and blistering heat on occasion. We then look at each other again, nod, and walk down the same side of the street, sharing the hoodrat edging burden as the junior high school thugs crossed to the right out of our way and begin aggressing against each other instead of us, like Daniel Boone and Mingo sliding by an under-strength party of Shawnee. If only all law and order broke down, these punks could be left in heaps where they belong. But the police—their reluctant protectors—still make their presence known.

Dan never went to the wilderness without his rifle. And into this government sponsored wilderness, where the only weapons permitted us are the lonely debris of this crumbling blight-by-design, one must always note the weapon caches and defensive strong points [doorways, narrow alleys, trash cans, etc.] and keep foremost in one's mind, that just as the hoodrat hunts you, you hunt it.

The animal which does not hunt is prey.

Don't be the prey.

'Niggely Bears'
Tommy Sotomayor Discusses the Thirteen Violent Percent

© 2016 James LaFond

Last night, after dark, and a trip down to the Hoodmart to get groceries, the streets were full of people, children, drunken teens, yelling and arguing, postponing the first open window rest of the dying winter. Last winter, when the weather broke, it was not like this. We did not have mobs of hoodrats occupying secondary street sidewalks, congregating in the middle of side streets.

So, I turned on YouTube...

How Savage Are Blacks In America & Why Is Everyone Afraid To Discuss It?

This is Tommy at his best.

"It acts, it doesn't think."

"The retribution of niggas."

Tommy exposes the criminal black as the slave bully of the liberal white elite. While many are afraid of black superman, it would only take a handful of real paleface men to solve this problem, which points up the fact, that we are really all afraid of the liberal White Daddy, who can take our job, our reputation and our freedom at the speed of the spoken word.

By the way, the picture on the video link below was taken ten months ago in my home town, on North Avenue. None of these people were arrested, charged or sought by authorities, telling me that they were doing White Daddy's bidding.

https://www.youtube.com/watch?v=QwCCj8Dx-gk

Black Lives Matter at McHoodrats

White Daddy's Bullies are Getting Warmed up For Purge Season

© 2016 James LaFond

"The carnival continues...

"And BTW, you won't find it in the Washington Post hard copy (they've finally been shamed into putting on their online version):"

-Samuel

http://www.dailymail.co.uk/news/article-3450254/Decorated-Iraq-vet-bravery-inspired-statues-says-beaten-teens-asked-black-lives-matter.html

Thanks for the link and the heads up Samuel. This is the only way I get news since my head is shoved up my keyboard's ass all week long...

The linked news story above happened thirty miles down the road in the nation's capital, which has a very violent culture. This was not reported on TV or in print in Baltimore, even though about 50,000 Baltimoreans work in and around D.C. This is the first half of the future. The second half is what happens to the next Iraqi war vet id he successfully defends against a gang of hood rats. He will be prosecuted to the fullest extent of the media. The liberal White Daddy is setting his two-legged dogs loose, so get used to it.

I was threatened twice in the past three days for the crime of not fearing blacks. This is one of the reasons why I occasionally eat at a McHoodrats, just so I can remind them that some palefaces do not live in fear.

'Where is the Most Rape Danger?'

An Answer for Julian on Baltimore Rape and How to Prevent It

© 2016 James LaFond

According to the FBI, most rapes are not reported, and all rapes are down since 1993. I have no idea how these two numbers coexist.

College rape alternately looks like an elaborate hoax or a vaginal holocaust, depending on the report cited.

Roughly a third of rapes take place in the home of the rapist, which means that was someone you know, unless they are a celebrity serial killer.

Roughly one quarter of rapes take place in the home of the victim, and are often stranger rapes, the most feared. [There is a separate category for rapes in a cohabitation zone.]

You will note that the area where most rapes are reported in Baltimore is the Northeast, where I live. I have not had sex with these women! This has to do with the fact that slightly more than half of the women are white and that black men from the Northeast and other areas do a lot of door kicking. The second highest area is the Southern district, home to upscale white women in their jogging prime. The ridiculous 2013 FBI stat, which will certainly be buried in the future, that had black on white interracial rapes to white on black rapes at about 13,000 to 2.5, comes to mind.

Where is the lowest incidence of rape?

With less than half the incidence of rape, the Northwestern and Southwestern— almost entirely black—districts hold the key to rape prevention:

1. You cannot rape the willing

2. 450-pound black women are hard to rape

3. When a 450-pound black woman rapes a 160-pound brutha, he is disinclined to report it!

So, Julian, the key is to wake op in the morning, look in the mirror and discover that you are now large, melanin enriched and in charge!

https://data.baltimorecity.gov/Public-Safety/2014-Rapes/gpc2-j5iy

Hoodrat Handball!
Baltimore City Police Department in Training for New Olympic Event!

© 2016 James LaFond

"So is this normal? And if so how is this cop not dead!?"

-Inspector Ratchet

Thanks for the heads up, Inspector.

This is what the cop's mother did to him.

This is what the hoodrat's mother has probably done to him since age two. Note how calm he remained, and how steady—well-versed in the fitted-hat shield defense.

This is what the female cop behind the gorilla cop most likely does to her offspring.

So yes, this is normal.

Why is the cop not dead?

Because the pig did not do this to my son.

However, once he is relieved of his civic duty and begins collecting unemployment, a few cousins or uncles might relieve us of the burden of continuing to feed him New York Fried Chicken 14 times a week.

This might seem trivial, but I also have a problem with the way the cop spoke to the youth. Exactly what portion of BPD Academy studies is devoted to learning the command uttered in the video?

On a technical note, the pivot was poorly executed, resulting in unnecessary follow through, which could have easily gotten him stabbed doing this as a bouncer or thug.

https://www.youtube.com/watch?v=N432rb
vCeyo

Hoodrat Handball, Civilian League
Tryouts at a Harm City Grocer Near You

© 2016 James LaFond

After viewing the video of our protect-and-serve poster child swatting that hoodrat around a Baltimore school hallway, I thought I should check with Megan down at the Harm City Gourmet Pork Rinds Emporium as to the latest up-and-coming hoodrat handball standouts.

Upon the arrival of the celebrity Ghetto Grocer in their midst, Arneesha and Kelly informed me that Megan was off. So I put the question to Kelly, who gave me the short version:

"Last night, about eight o'clock, this customer—petite, about twenty—was looking for her two-year-old, a really adorable little kid who is at that stage where he just wants to run around with his hands in the air. You can hear him running down the aisles giggling and hear her yelling, 'Dashawntay, yo betta get yo muvafucin' ass up in dis bitch or I'll whoop da shit outta you!'

"She was totally ghetto. So I send security [the Nigerian guard who recently risked life and limb snatching a two-pound pack of frozen burgers out from between the ginormous breastesses of a fashionably dressed 450-pound shoplifter] to get the kid. Somehow the kid has climbed under a freezer case or end cap or something and the security guard is dragging him out. But when he sets him on his feet he's off to the races, headed for the front door—which is swinging open—and we all hold our breath.

"But the kid dove behind it just before he got smashed, which enabled the guard to disable the door and hand the kid out to his mother, who immediately grabbed him by one arm, held him out like a piñata and starts waking him so hard that he's spinning around while he's crying and she's screaming muva this and bitch that. She even called him the n-word.

"Just another night in the hood, baby."

Something New Under the Dark Sun

The Violence Guy is Surprised on a Harm City Sidewalk

I walked past a hoodrat trail today, a beaten path across a marginal, unused space, close to two occupied mansions, and one unoccupied vacant farm house with shed and barn, that somehow got swallowed by this cancerous city. Unknown to the police and to most of the area residents, this is a place where youth criminals gather to organize, to parlay, to head out on raiding parties, to initiate set members.

In the past five years I have found many things here: a revolver cylinder for a .38 caliber hand gun, a broken pocket knife, hair, blood, and all of the assorted markings of our high culture—crack vials, liquor bottles, needles. It is my policy never to touch anything in this quarter acre, but to view it from various angles and try and reconstruct the nocturnal goings on here, which I do try to avoid witnessing.

Today, at 3:43 on this Thursday afternoon, as a cold storm front rolled in overhead, I found something new under the sun, which does not occur often for me in this line of inquiry.

At my feet, on the curb, precisely the size of my 8.5 sneaker, was the body of a Norway rat, with a rubbery 11-inch tail, as thick as my smallest finger at the base. The rat was killed last night, by some means which did not involve bloodshed but did deform the skull. This rat was posed, to lay on its back like a slain human, a post-mortem posturing artifice that had turned half way into the normal rodent fetal position.

On this large, boss rat's chest, was—still is, I think, as it has been less than two hours—a 4G smart phone, the screen having been cracked in a starburst pattern by what I presume was the glass-breaking spike on a tactical folding knife, of the kind on sale for $5 down the street at the Pakistani convenience store. This smart phone covered the mid-portion of the rat's body, making him something of the picture-frame to this gruesome work of art, which I do understood, could have accidentally occurred due to a convergence of plausible factors that have nothing to do with hoodrats sending some kind of anti-snitching method. However, the use of dead rats to warn associates against cooperating with the authorities is so pervasive in Baltimore, that cops do it to each other.

I do not believe it is a stretch to surmise that a local youth thug will be sweating pretty profusely on this wintery night.

'Bullying'
Tommy Sotomayor Describes the Death of Innocence

© 2016 James LaFond

In the last two minutes Tommy gets down to the core issue faced by all children in our age-segregated and racially-polarized society, a threat that hits black children the hardest, and then hits the other races they interact with by way of the resulting hateful expression.

One of the skills I developed as the ghetto grocer was "putting paper on people," documenting every workplace transgression so that I would be able to terminate them for threatening coworkers—fellow black coworkers. Firing a person for a pattern of harassment is very difficult to do and avoid paying their unemployment. The number of times middle-aged men threatened violence against coworkers for trivial things was astonishing. So, when Jetty called up Nelson and left him a threatening voicemail, I fired him for the cookies he didn't rotate, three weeks in a row, not for the voicemail I never listened to while standing in front of the #10 can green been display.

I understand Tommy a lot better now.

This video was taken down, which is the fate of many of Tommy's thousands of videos, as he is under intense racial pressure, including death threats, from blacks.

The Hunted

Reading Predatory Urban Sign through Prey Behavior

It has been some time since I have examined bus use patterns. Mass transit is very susceptible to any type of social disruption, often faring worse during social upheaval than during natural disasters and winter weather events.

On the bus, I mostly sleep with my sunglasses and hood on.

I am taking a Wednesday night on one bus line as a sample, as Monday and Friday, the other two days I typically use the bus, are more prone to irregularities such as holidays, drivers staying home to watch the Monday Night Football game, etc.

Habitat Hoodrat: Ho-Nation

This concerns only predation, not social vetting brawls between hoodrat breeders.

In Baltimore, there are now three* types of predators, from most to least likely to attack:

1. Hoodrats

2. Pigs

3. Fatheads*

The Prey Species of Habitat Hoodrat are, from most to least often attacked:

1. Hoodrats

2. Palefaces

3. Fatheads

4. Slanteyes

*These are Salvadorans come through Mexico and up into Baltimore to prey on Mexican dishwashers and such. Machete attacks are now on the rise in East Baltimore, according to my confidential Latin sources. It appears that Donald Trump was right about Latinos coming to Baltimore to commit crime. He must be psychic, because it wasn't going on last year.

Changes in Behavior of Prey Species After Dark

1. Hoodrats are taking the bus at half the frequency as they did before the Purge [which targeted whites predominantly] they are also not walking back into the neighborhoods, but waiting for another bus, a cab, a hack, or an escort to come and get them. Within 200 yards of the bus stop I use at night, four houses have gone up for sale, two owned by blacks, two by whites.

2. Palefaces are taking the bus in half the numbers, but are all males—where the hoodrats are half female—and are walking back in the neighborhoods. However, no paleface is using bus stops in the Rosedale-Essex area where the hoodrat hunt for palefaces was in full swing during the Purge, with this paleface being a notable exception to the paleface rabbit rule. The palefaces only take the bus from Towson to Overlea, and no longer venture further east, where thousands of Harm City Hoodrats [which have noticeably more pronounced tails than Harm County Hoodrats] have been imported over the last four years.

3. Fatheads are no longer taking the bus at night. Since these are higher earners than hoodrats and palefaces, I suspect they have bought cars or are taking sedans and cabs.

4. No slanteyes—a delicacy in Harm County and Harm City to begin with—are taking the bus at night.

This is just one line. But, this is a county-to-county line that straddles numerous city and county police precincts and is known to be one of the safest bus lines in the Greater Baltimore Metropolitan Area. I will examine traditionally more dangerous bus routes at another time. Keep in mind, that the #55 links three of these, and that the bus stop behavior at the major transfer points holds for users of all lines. People are very conscious that they will be hunted as they leave a bus stop and are taking prudent precautions. Behavior on the bus is much less friendly, and much more quite as well, with a reduction in bad behavior and civility at the same time, with people tending toward a generally none-threatening, anti-social demeanor.

The Black Terminatrix Hierarchy

7th Grade BT-1100 Brawls With Skynet BT-900 Teacher In Detroit Cyberdyne Training Facility

© 2016 James LaFond

When I was a kid I always looked forward to monster battles on TV: Godzilla versus King Kong, T-Rex versus Triceritops.

I never imagined I'd get such a treat as an adult—no less on a regular basis. Also, on a technical note, Tommy fills the viewer in on the Black Terminatrix hierarchy.

Crack open a beer and enjoy.

https://www.youtube.com/watch?v=AXV2rItZyiQ

In Search of the Literate BT-1000

Nero the Pict Researches Black Terminatrix Literacy Initiative on Yo Tube

© 2016 James LaFond

"You might want to check the link to this oldie but goody. It features similar (but seemingly justified) antics over at the Pratt branch [library] on Orleans Street. Oh, and the "teen" slapee is female. The TV interview with the "teen's" brother and cousin is priceless.'

-Nero the Pict

http://www.wbaltv.com/news/library-fight-between-teen-security-officer-caught-on-video/25190284

First, I have a comment.

Are Baltimore news anchors cast by pornography producers?

Why must it always be a black man and a white woman, usually a blonde?

Never a white man and a white woman.

Never a black man and a black woman.

Never a white man and a black woman.

How about a white dude and an obedient Latina—I might watch that news cast.

The white men are all slotted for sports and weather, with Asian chicks and black women doing human interest, traffic, etc.

Okay, Nero, as a man who did much research at the Central Branch, our Hero Cop here is being properly reassigned. The

Central Branch of the Pratt Library, the repository of much historic literature, is swarmed by platoon strength mobs of homeless men every morning. The men's room is behind bars and safety glass. Armed cops herd these vagrants like correction officers. I had them yell at me a few times. This man has the right stuff!

I loved the smirks on these two goof relatives of hers. You knew they were happy to find out that the bitch that has terrorized them since they were toddlers was finally smacked down, but if they had said otherwise there would have been "Hell ta pay, nigga!"

For all of you rural whites that think that blacks in cities are tough, know that more often than not, it is the opposite. Look at these two sissies—this is what women produce when they father children. That's why the authorities will increasingly be backing up hoodrats who attack lab rats, because the mob is mostly fluffy prancers.

The second punk almost broke into laughter when he referred to her as a "lady!"

Notice, after all police and hoodrat violence, and hoodrat versus lab rat violence that results in a favorable outcome for the lab rat, that the hoodrats always call for prison time for the non-hoodrat.

They own the system, and know it.

Why shouldn't they? After all, it was designed for them.

'Why You Don't See Blacks Camping'

10 Black Things Liberals just Don't Understand by Gavin McInnes

"James, I think there is a smattering of the truth in this one."

- Ronald

http://takimag.com/article/10_black_thing s_liberals_just_dont_understand_gavin_mc innes/print#axzz41t5z4jAZ

Thanks for this, Ronald. As a Baltimorean, I'm sure it nags at your mind that the people who are constantly speaking on behalf of our black neighbors never seem to have met one and are the first people to avoid contact with blacks, particularly non-celebrity blacks. The fact is liberals care about black folks about as much as some black thug cares about the pit bull he is feeding that poodle to on bait night—a poodle that the liberal owner thinks ran away, but has been snatched from her yard by a sixteen-year-old who has no greater ambition in life than to be feared by the weakest among us.

That said, the best reason to read this article, is that it is hilarious!

'Ass-Kickin' Good'
DC Teen Killed By Niggly Bear Over A Piece Of Chicken!

" I Guess Black Lives Don't Matter To Niggaz!"

-Tommy Soyomayor

It is Sunday morning, folks, time for our weekly communion with the greater angels of our nature. Once upon a "hawngray" time in Harm City, Duz was grilling in his backyard when a dude took the last rib off the girl across the alley and got his head split open by a beastly babe with a beer bottle, bringing on a general brawl. In this vide Tommy covers a similar, but more lethal, story from "fiddy" miles down the road, in the nation's moral heart, Washington D.C.

Now, in all solemn seriousness, let's say a prayer for the deceased, that his eternal berth happens to be alongside that of Colonel Sanders.

https://www.youtube.com/watch?v=ypqyNoF9vLo

More Hoodrats, Mom, Please!
Baltimore County Settles Federal U.S. Bias Complaint, Will Spend 30 Million To Bring Crime to Suburbs

© 2016 James LaFond

So scream the liberal slaves of the Mamma State.

On the same day that we discover that the Freddie Gray martyrdom trials will resume in May, with the persecution of a cop with an appropriately Roman name of Nero—I think Nero stabbed Freddie in the side with his pilum while the other cops rolled dice for his sneakers—the news, sorry, I meant "good news" henceforth rendered "gospel" on Tuesday, 3/15/16, that Baltimore County has settled with the feds over the crime of not having enough low income housing in middleclass neighborhoods hit the suburban mouth like a festering cold sore.

Habitat Hoodrat: Ho-Nation

One of the neighborhoods, is Cockeysville, where preppers were moving twenty years ago, and where one of my black fighters is paying high rent in order to keep his children away from criminal black elements. Things should go smoothly here, as the county had the foresight to set up a methadone clinic there a few years ago.

Now all of the white rabbits who fled the low-intensity black-on-white race war of 1980s Baltimore will have to move again! Recently when advising my son on buying house, I told him to stay closer to the city rather than in the prime retail and housing zones, as these were in the federal cross hairs for blacksploitation. The detonation was read, not heard, but the force of the blast will ripple for twenty years.

When buying a house, if you can afford it, you must go rural, where there is no infrastructure. Anyplace where strip malls are popping up, where Wal-marts are rising, will become a low income hoodrat hatchery. The suburbs are doomed. Go rural or stay urban, where you at least have structurally defensible enclaves, as opposed to getting caught in the suburban net that was designed to put you at the mercy of teenage criminals when you are in your eighties.

Habitat Hoodrat: Ho-Nation

Look at a suburban McMansion and compare it ot an old city row house. It is like comparing a tent to a bunker. The only ultimately survivable setting in case things go way into the cosmic toilet is rural. In the mean time, while sweating in Sodom, you might choose to live behind walls and doors that can hold up to a sneaker.

If you are a White Marsh, Towson or Cockeysville home buyer, welcome to the meat chute of souls, thoughtfully paved to ease your digestibility.

Ambushing Cops in P.G. County, MD

A Would Be YouTube GangstaBlamDaPoleeseDrama Goes Lame

I pay little attention to local news, and rely on word of mouth, my own experiences and observations and a few sets of prying eyes to give me the heads up. Apparently a band of incompetent brothers decided to record their own death by cop but got arrested instead, with the only slain cop being taken down by friendly fire. It seems that the raid fell somewhat short of the police precinct gunfight in The Terminator.

There are some links below.

If you are a regular Harm City reader, keep in mind that The Mac Daddy, Big Gus, and Big Daddy Dee were all "P.G. County niggas." It is interesting, that although Baltimore gets so much violent press, that Prince Georges County, which is D.C. suburban, is a place most feared by Baltimore blacks, it having a reputation as bad as D.C. itself. Key stories of a very brutal nature occurring in P.G. County are to be found in When You're Food and The Logic of Steel.

http://baltimore.cbslocal.com/2016/03/15/brothers-accused-in-recording-attack-that-left-officer-dead/

http://baltimore.cbslocal.com/show/cbs-baltimore-live-video/video-3373752-two-brothers-charged-in-firefight-that-lead-to-pr-georges-officers-death/

http://baltimore.cbslocal.com/show/cbs-baltimore-live-video/video-3373621-wjz-your-desk-march-15-2016/

Nick's Day
Getting Stuck Up on the Way to Work

© 2016 James LaFond

Saint Patrick's Day, 3/17/16

A former black coworker of mine was leaving for work yesterday morning, turning the corner from Penn onto North Avenue at 10 a.m. on a sunny early spring day, on a primary street shared with the Northeast District Courthouse, when a younger, innocent, unarmed, black man, wearing a ski-cap on this 80 degree day, pulled it down over his face into a ski-mask, came face-to-face with him on the sidewalk, presented a gun from a close draw [holding the bent elbow of his gun hand close to his ribs] pointed at Nick's belly, and said, "Empty yo pockets, yo."

Nick turned out his pockets, which contained his keys, a stick of gum, his cell phone, and one dollar and twenty seven cents he had pocketed to buy a soda at work.

He was then told, with a wave of the handgun [an automatic of a type he could not identify, which seemed kind of small to him], "Walk on, yo—git up da way."

As he resumed his walk to work, an effort that would not cover the replacement of the phone, his keys rattled down the sidewalk behind him, so he turned tentatively and picked them up as the robber jogged away down the sidewalk.

Nick made it to work on time and his manager bought him a soda.

Nick's day was a typical day in the life of a working black man living among black criminals, a secret life with no meaning, for Nick's terrorized life does not matter, unless, of course, it is taken by a white man. But since Nick is a working man, and gives himself precious few opportunities to fight police officers and does not attack white men, it is very unlikely that he will ever matter in Urban Plantation America.

Habitat Hoodrat: Ho-Nation
Print Title: 2016-9

For the low brow, investigative comedy that is much of the Harm City genre I have decided to continue Habitat Hoodrat as a series, beginning with Habitat Hoodrat: Ho-Nation, which shall, of course, by followed by Yo-Nation, Retard-Nation, etc.

I have commissioned a cover from a black friend of mine, and given him three days to get it to me. I hope he makes the deadline in my rampant mind so that I will be able to credit a victim of my pale privilege with the insulting graphics I have in mind. He and I discussed the possibility that I might be hauled before Congress in pink breast cancer awareness chains and put on trial before Oprah and assorted dykes, white faggots, emasculated negroes and mouthy hos, for my literary crimes.

Oliver said, "James, I would very much like to see that congressional hearing."

I responded, "See it—Bro? You'd be in it, as my character witness, my 'black friend,' though I presume I'd have a hard time explaining away the fact that I beat you with a stick..."

Look for Habitat Hoodrat: Ho-Nation this coming week.

When Labrats Attack!
The New Emasculation Paradigm in White Suburbia

© 2016 James LaFond

The whiggers are back with a thirst to be as feared as the black hoodrat heroes of urban myth and media legend. Why be a standup, old-school redneck when you can cock that fitted hat sideways, quote Kid Rock or Eminem and pack up with other savage pussies to cover your sissy self with the patina of manhood?

Recently Greg, who is a loud mouth, a dick and a little obnoxious when he gets drunk, but is not known to beat people up and has no street cred as a badass or any such type, but simply a trash talker, was at the Emerald Tavern, a sports bar in Baltimore County where Mescaline Franklin and I have shared drinks before. While at the bar, Greg said something complimentary about the appearance of a woman, who happened to be there with her boyfriend and his three buddies. All parties were 21-23, in a bar that usually caters to a thirty something crowd.

When Greg went to the men's room all four guys followed him in and beat him for perhaps five minutes. I saw the photos of his face and it was bad. He had not been punched much, mostly having his face smashed against hard objects and scraped on walls.

When I was a young man coming up, there were one solid difference between white guys and blacks, and every black guy and every white guy would tell you how it was. White guys would fight you straight up, but black guys would always gang up on you.

The manner of Greg's beating is one of many recent indications I have seen that the functionally absent white father in suburbia and the lionizing of black men as the masculine standard is beginning to rot the Caucasian soul in adolescence, producing white youth who are increasingly indistinguishable in behavior from their sainted and underprivileged counter parts from the media's preferred racial group.

Nice Nick
A Few Notes on Real Gentle Giants

© 2016 James LaFond

Recently I told the brief story of Nick, being robbed at gunpoint by another black man on his way to his poverty-level job. In retrospect, I considered this event, which was related to me by Nick's boss, who phoned in the account—a conservative white man who wants to make sure that this crack pot lets his readers know that his black help is preyed upon by black criminals. I know the feeling.

I would like to say a little more about Nick here. The first thing you would notice about Nick as that he is a big, big guy, six-four and 370.

The second thing you would notice about him is that he, like most really big black guys, is, in fact, a gentle giant. Those that are not gentle go into working in contact sports and security and law enforcement. For this reason, on the surface of it, Tiny Teen from Yo Town Illinois was assumed by many blacks around the country to have been a gentle giant upon first hearing about the shooting and hearing those two words, so often used in the ghetto. And, as their liberal slave masters know, once stupid emotive people come to believe a thing in a moment, they will rarely part with that belief, particularly if their life experience is in line with that belief.

First of all, let's speak of big guys. Big men are usually less aggressive than small men as adults. One need only follow boxing to note how rare hyper-aggressive big men are, and why they are such a terror when they emerge in the heavy ranks.

In the white community big men generally have little experience with aggression, as they get bullied but rarely by their peer group as they come along in age-ranked classes and then go home to friends and family.

In the black community school is never the focus of childhood life—simply a temporary prison stay, preparing them for a life in and out of such institutions. When they go home they are ignored, rejected and brutalized by their mother.

There is no father—this being the crucial accomplishment of liberalism in America, the generation of a fatherless 13% that might look to Uncle Sam as their Daddy.

Now the child is living on the street, where as many as thirty kids to a block mill around amongst youth and young men from drug gangs. These are un-parented children and youth ranging in age from 5-17. What happens in this setting to the extra-large boy is he is brutally beaten by older girls and older boys as he is used for practice, and to break him into a lackey stooge for corner work, just being marked as a potential meat shield.

Out of every four big boys you can generalize and say that this produces one of each of the following type with regularity:

1. Timid, emasculated teddy bears like Nice Nick who walk with down cast eyes and mumble.

2. Obedient, emasculated, beta males who follow the lead of the smaller more aggressive men and women who take control of their life and who will only participate in group attacks, or to "defend" their violent wife/mother/girl/sister and not with enthusiasm.

3. Big emasculated, nerds, geeks and good boys who get as far away from the black community as they can and associate with whites as much as possible. Many gravitate to private security work in passive roles and to sedentary activities with other racial groups. The ones that stay in the black hood that conform to this type will typically get into bootleg clothes, shoe and DVD vending and make an art out of making friends and not making enemies.

4. Big psychopaths like Mike Brown, who, if they have brains go into sports or work as doormen at strip clubs, and if not, end up being meat-shields for drug gangs. Note that in Mike Brown's case he was led into the situation that got him killed by a smaller, older, experienced criminal.

So, the myth of the "gentle giant" is based on fact, and is generally a rule to live by in bad places, as long as you keep your eye out for the exception— because that dude is bad news.

Getting the Axe
A Latino View of African American Civility

© 2016 James LaFond

Two weeks ago Raphael was at bar in East Baltimore—a night club that caters to all ethnicities and is worked by a squad of big black bouncers. As the bouncers looked on with humorous smirks, a loud mouthed, stocky, black dude began threatening another black dude, with lots of talk back and forth. The short aggressive guy took a low boxing stance and the taller fit guy took a relaxed stance without his hands up. As they talked trash the short guy kept getting lower and lower into his weird boxing crouch.

After a full minute of trash talking and posturing the short guy said, "Bring it, Yo."

To this the taller man—who Raphael all of a sudden recalled was a taekwondo instructor—brought his Timberland boot up high over head and brought it down in an ax kick that planted the heel on the shoulder blade and the toe on the face, dropping the drunken-yo-fu superstar in front of the bar.

I'll let Raphael take it from here:

"Of course, they're all black, so they gotta keep talking shit—like it's some kind of law or something. Now the taekwondo man is running his mouth. The bouncers scraped this piece-of-you-know-what up and tell him to leave, but they let the other guy stay because he didn't start it."

It must be nice to be a taekwondo guy and have some guy not only pick a fight with you but squat down and give you a chance to look like Andy Hug.

Miss Ginger
An Old School Baltimore Woman Behind the Collective Wheel

© 2016 James LaFond

This past Thursday morning, as I took the #55 home, piloted by Ginger, who is a handsome fifty-year-old black women with her own neatly combed and oiled hair, who has not gained the African American weight stipulated by liberal law, in order to keep diabetic clinics busy, was her normally effusive self. She supervises the boarding of the bus, everyone's time precious to her. She is the best bus driver the MTA has and is especially protective of white folks who still venture onto her coach, making sure by the tone in her voice that the hoodrats listening know that she'll tell the cops the truth if they jack up one of "my white people."

On Kenwood Avenue, a block from where numerous gang stompings by black mobs against white individuals have recently occurred, a twelve year old white boy boarded. He appeared to be five-feet two-inches and weigh about 80 pounds. He was dressed to go to prep school. He had obviously not boarded a bus before, so Ginger stopped him and the coach, and said loud enough for everyone to hear, "Baby, are you going to take this bus regularly?"

I looked around to see if any of the hoodrat wannabes who have been making noise about busting me up are around, and they are not. I was pissed at his parents, when he nodded "yes," as I may very well end up going to jail over him if he ever boards a bus occupied by me and not piloted by Ginger.

Ginger then gave him her New White Passenger Speech, modified for his age:

"Baby, Miss Ginger will see you, so don't go stepping out to get my attention. This is a big coach. Wave if you want. I will stop for you. Now where are you getting off?"

After the boy told her, she said, "Baby, I will not let you miss your stop. Sit right here behind me, and remember, Miss Ginger has your back, Baby.'

She then looked up into the mirror at the junior high school and high school kids on the back deck and said, "You all heard that, didn't you? That's right, Miss Ginger's Baby Boy here is having a nice safe MTA experience."

The boy was ushered off with much pomp and deference by his ebony mother dowager a stop before mine. He did get up the voice to thank her in a little cracking chirp as he stepped off.

I then stepped up behind Ginger and asked for the next stop, and she said, "You've got it, Sir."

It may seem a small thing to the reader. But that little exchange, followed by my thanking her and her telling me, "I know *you* have a safe walk, Sir," was basically Ginger's way of letting me know, that since she was going to be "witnessing white" during the coming troubles, that she expected me to fight the entire NBA if necessary, to keep any passengers she rated as non-combatants from being beat up on her coach or on an adjacent stop.

It occurred to me that this is how men and women should interact in the face of tyranny, according to a set of expectations that one will stand up to the animals set loose on us, and the other will speak the truth to our mutual master.

10,000 Miss Gingers is all it would take to civilize this 100,000 hoodrat shithole. Unfortunately her model has been discontinued.

Edging Out Hoodrats
On the Sidewalk with Three Wannabe Gs

© 2016 James LaFond

This past Friday afternoon, at 4:10 p.m., I was walking away from the liquor store in Baynesville, after coaching Mister Ben for an hour at the school. He gave me an extra twenty, so I bought some high-end microwbrew from Pottstown PA, and was looking forward to enjoying a few with a friend, before taking my pre-work nap.

I passed the row of brick-faced duplex rentals, a tiny transplanted ghetto setting where an unemployed adult black man between 30 and 60 sits on each porch and never give me any cause for concern. These are guys produced by the worst ghettos in Baltimore, City, who somehow survived and are hoping to quietly end their days out here in the County. A large man of about my age, but much more worn and droopy-eyed, held up a big hand and said, in a slurred, but kindly voice, "Have a blessed day, Sir."

The street I am walking along leads back to the gas station, liquor store and bus stop, and joins Loch Raven Blvd. at the Whiz carwash, across the street from the Raven Inn, where I met Uncle Bernie for a burger yesterday. This side street is the tap that empties the pedestrian elements of the neighborhood onto the main drag. The fact that this liquor store is doing well a quarter mile from the biggest and best liquor store in Maryland, is proof positive that very many of these row houses have been rented by pedestrians and mass transit users. Their single serve selection is twice normal for a County outlet. The numerous for sale signs by white owners are the rest of the proof. I advised my son against buying this far out, and he purchased a place in an area that has been bypassed by this a mile down the road.

Approaching me on the sidewalk are three 17-year-old, innocent, unarmed, black youths, all standing over six feet, and all fit. One is walking behind and two are walking in front. I move to the right side of the sidewalk and continue, not wanting to waste the $12 six pack of cans on one of those unworthy skulls, as it is intended to degrade the contents of my own skull.

Instead of going single file as I switch the beer bag to the right hand, they spread out, shoulder to shoulder, with the most muscular boy, that was in back, walking in the grass to my right, meaning I've got to climb the bank to the left or go out into the street to the right, or go through.

I'm going through. My shoulder height is perfect for a butt into a solar plexus of these tall, slim hoodrats, who are well-dressed, gaudily-shoed, and smart-phoned up to $400, wearing gold chains, and speaking standard English?

These are wannabe gees, middleclass suburban kids who have imbibed the media worship of ghetto blacks and want that status for themselves. The real ghetto guys are sitting up on the porches shaking their heads, looking at a local reenactment of the type of behavior they have recently fled—waiting for them to show up, and then drive off the white people they hoped to live with, because white people do not attack you!

I only know this because the Jesus-guy on the porch groans at the aggressive pack formation in response to my courtesy.

My eyes are on the chests, open wide behind my sunglasses to detect elbow movement. If an elbow moves my left shoulder goes into the center solar plexus and I break through and flail with the six-pack of cans in the plastic sack. If this fails, I have a knife.

Just as my right shoulder is about to hit the muscle guy in the wind, he loses his cool and skips like a faggot between me and the middle guy, even giving a girly "woo-woo" sound—from Shaft to Peter Pan in one second.

Dude, on behalf of masculine kind, that was embarrassing. I'd respect you more if you had tried to punch me.

In Habitat Hoodrat it's raining sissies again.

Perhaps I'll befriend one of these ex-criminals on the rental porches and exchange a cold one for a story one Friday afternoon, and talk about the bad old days, back when a homeboy had the balls to go through with a bad idea.

This is James "Still the White Devil" LaFond, reporting on the Harm City infestation.

It is spreading but weak. A few tough white cells might be all you need in the absence of a federally approved vaccine.

Hamilton, Northeast Baltimore, 3/21/16

The End

www.ingramcontent.com/pod-product-compliance
Lightning Source LLC
Chambersburg PA
CBHW070831310526
45788CB00017B/455